IJALA

IJALA

SONIA SANCHEZ AND
THE AFRICAN POETIC TRADITION

Joyce A. Joyce

Third World Press
Chicago

Third World Press, Chicago 60619

Printed in the United States of America.

05 04 03 02 01 00 99 98 97 96   5 4 3 2 1

Cover Photo by Marion Ettlinger

Library of Congress Cataloging-in-Publication Data

Joyce, Joyce Ann, 1949-
      Ijala: Sonia Sanchez and the African Poetic
Tradition / Joyce A. Joyce.
            p.   cm.
      Includes bibliographical references.
      ISBN: 0-88378-190-5 (hardcover)
                  0-88378-189-1 (paper).
      1. Sanchez, Sonia, 1935-   ---Criticism and
interpretation. 2. Women and literature---United
States---History---20th century. 3. American poetry---
African influences. 4. Afro-American women in
literature. 5. Afro-Americans in literature. I. Title.
PS3569.A468Z73   1996
811'.54--dc21
                                                    96-47609
                                                         CIP

DEDICATION

To Gwendolyn Brooks,
Dudley Randall,
and Margaret Walker

EPIGRAPH

I am always enamored of the craft of poetry. When you get lost in that craft or form, you come out smiling. It's like that first moment of making love. It's the same kind of thing as being in the classroom and making a point and seeing the students get it. It's that kind of joy.

Sonia Sanchez

CONTENTS

PREFACE

In the early 1980s, Professor Erlene Stetson asked me to choose a Black woman writer I would like to write a critical essay on for "Black Sister II," a proposed collection of essays addressing the various women writers in her volume *Black Sister: Poetry by Black American Women*, 1746-1980 (1981). Although Professor Stetson was unable to complete this project, I profited greatly from my choice of Sonia Sanchez and the research I began on her poetry. The essay I prepared for Professor Stetson entitled "The Development of Sonia Sanchez: A Continuing Journey" was published in the *Indian Journal of American Studies*, 13, 2 (July 1983). Third World Press suggested that the above essay, which critically examines Sonia Sanchez' poetry from her first collection *Home Coming* (1969) to her collection *I've Been a Woman: New and Selected Poems* (1978), should be included in the present study that explores the development and source of Sanchez' poetic genius. Another of my essays on Sanchez, "Sonia Sanchez and T. S. Eliot," was included in my last book *Warriors, Conjurers, and Priests: Defining African-centered Literary Criticism* (1994).

This study then reflects fifteen years in which I have studied Sonia Sanchez' poetry, taught her poetry in the classroom, and attended her poetry performances. As I hope the introduction and the essay "The Continuing Journey of Sonia Sanchez: *from homegirls and handgrenades* to *Wounded in the House of a Friend*" that follow will show, I have grappled with the complexity of Sanchez' art. I have observed her maturation as a poet and the diversity of her work. The purpose of the chapter "Bantu, Nkodi, Ndungu, and Nganga: Language, Politics, Music, & Religion in African-American Poetry" is to place Sanchez in the

African-American poetic tradition through a theoretical reading of African-American poetry, providing an overview of Sanchez' precursors as well as contemporaries, and suggesting the direction of African-American poetry.

An integral relationship exists between the title of this entire study "Ijala: Sonia Sanchez and the African Poetic Tradition" and the theoretical chapter "Bantu, Nkodi, Ndungu, and Nganga." A key issue that I raised in my first essay on Sanchez and again more fully in *Warriors, Conjurers, and Priests* involves the historical inclination of African-American writers, both creative writers and critics, to use Eurocentric writers and their aesthetic as the models of excellence. In "Bantu, Nkodi, Ndungu, and Nganga," I suggest that we look inside the works and culture of African-American poets to deduce those aesthetic characteristics (both stylistic and thematic) that distinguish African-American poetry. The terms (bantu, nkodi, ndungu, and nganga) I use for these distinguishing features are not only African in origin, they also reflect the interconnectedness between African artifacts (including language) and African daily life. Such interconnectedness is characteristic of African-American poetry from Phillis Wheatley to Sonia Sanchez, as well as their descendants—Ruth Forman, Kevin Powell, Ras Baraka, and D-Knowledge. These terms then suggest the grounding of African-American poetry in an African tradition that pervaded Black folk culture in the eighteenth and nineteenth centuries, which Stephen Henderson cites as the precursor for the type of poetry Sanchez and others began to publish in the late 1960s and early 1970s. What I do in "Bantu, Nkodi, Ndungu, and Nganga" is take Stephen Henderson's thesis back one step further from South Carolina, where the largest number of Bantu slaves were brought to America, to western and central Africa along the Congo River to the Bantu culture of the Bakongo.

While the characteristics of African-American poetry

that Stephen Henderson ingeniously details in his *Understanding the New Black Poetry* are valuable to my early explorations of Sanchez' poetry, I sensed over the last five years that some aspects of Sanchez' poetry were eluding me. My discovery of Nigerian scholar Isidore Okpewho's *African Oral Literature: Backgrounds, Characters, and Continuity* and of Mohamed H. Abdulaziz' study of the nineteenth-century Swahili poet Muyaka bin Haji brought these missing pieces into focus. *Ijala: Sonia Sanchez and the African Poetic Tradition* looks directly into the African poetic tradition where orality precedes the written form of poetry and where the two are inextricably intertwined.

Although the Yoruba have several words to define poetry according to the nature of the pitch of the poet's voice—*esa* or *ewa* for a falsetto voice; *rara* for a slow wailing, long drawn-out chanting style; *ofo* or *ogede* for magic formula sentences rapidly spoken in normal speech pattern; and *ijala* for a high-pitched voice—I chose *ijala* for the title of my study not only because it describes the nature of Sanchez' chants but also because *ijala* in traditional Yoruba culture is performed by hunters or devotees of Ogun, the Yoruba god of iron or war. Because Sanchez uses her voice to affect her listeners' emotions, and because she uses her poetry to fight social and political evils, I chose *ijala* to describe her place in the African poetic tradition by identifying her with the devotees of Ogun, the god of war.

In an interview with D. H. Melhem that appears in *Heroism in the New Black Poetry: Introductions & Interviews*, Sanchez cites Swahili praise poetry as an influence on her early work, particularly on the autobiographical poem *A Blues Book for Blue Black Magical Women* (1974). In the following essay, I shall discuss the characteristics of this poetry in relation to Sanchez' work. In the pamphlet *Crisis and Culture: Two Speeches by Sonia Sanchez* (1983), she again exhibits her knowledge of East African Islamic poets who wrote in Swahili when she quotes passages from two of such poets. The title of her first essay in *Crisis and Culture*, "The Poet as a Creator of Social Values," and her listing of the six characteristics of African liberation poetry near the end of that essay led to my use of Yoruba, Swahili, and Bantu in the exploration of her artistry. In the creation of social values, Sanchez contends that African liberation poetry must be functional (relate to people's struggle), inspirational (inspire the people to continue the struggle against oppression), educational (teach the people the what and the why of the struggle), instructional (prescribe help), idealogical [*sic*] (embrace the political ideology on which the struggle is based), and political (foster national consciousness and solidarity) (13-14). One of the most consistent aspects of African culture is the interconnectedness between art and people's lives. Regardless of the nature of the oral performance or poem (whether a love song, war song, praise song, patriotic song, marriage song, harvest song, initiation song, or eulogy), African poetry is a response to a cultural need. Thus, poetry and the six social functions it performs are inextricable according to Sanchez.

My use of *ijala* refers to the functional, inspirational, educational, instructional, ideological, and political nature of Sanchez' poetry, that is, her poetic war against various forms of oppression. Inherent in African liberation poetry is the importance of identity and heritage; the poet cannot create social values, nor can she instruct, inspire, or educate without a strong sense of self and without an equally strong connection with her history. In turn, the people who are to receive the poet's message profit most when they identify with the poet and connect their history with that of the poet's. Identity then is the key element in my use of Bantu words to describe the linguistic, political, musical, and religious nature of African-American poetry.

Although Sanchez' poetry is basically free of allusions to Christianity, in the 1970s she was, for a time, a member of the Nation of Islam. Islamic references pervade her autobiographical book-length poem *A Blues Book for Blue Black Magical Women*. Because I had not discovered Swahili-Islamic verse in the early 1980s, I did not explore this influence in the early essay "The Development of Sonia Sanchez: A Continuing Journey." The following essay will address the functional, educational, and aesthetic nature of this influence on Sanchez' poetry.

Because African-American poetry of the early 1970s that came out of the Black Arts Movement, such as Sonia Sanchez', is considered more rhetorical than artistically or aesthetically sound, "Bantu, Nkodi, Ndunga, and Nganga: Language, Politics, Music, & Religion in African-American Poetry" demonstrates that African-American poets have always created their own aesthetic while demonstrating great familiarity with a Eurocentric poetic form.

The essays that follow focus specifically on Sonia Sanchez. They examine the African origins of her stirring, emotional reading/performance and of her creative imagination that coins phrases such as "Under a Soprano Sky," "homegirls and handgrenades," "I shall become a collector of me," "smell the beginning," "whirlwinds of joy and rage," "braids of hurt," and many others that pervade her poetry from *Home Coming* (1969) to *Wounded in the House of a Friend* (1995).

ACKNOWLEDGMENTS

I would like to thank Haki R. Madhubuti and Third World Press for years of support. I am proud to have this book included in the Third World Press list.

I would also like to thank Denise King-Miller for her inspiration and faith in my ability to perform administrative duties and continue to write, as well as Ruby Essein, who edited the manuscript for me at a moment's notice.

And finally, I would like to thank my husband Walter R. Gholson III for his understanding, compassion, and support.

ERRATA

Page	For	Read
133, lines 1-2	Nicolas Galen, Pablo Narrate	Nicolas Guillen, Pablo Neruda
134, line 18	the air late this summer	the air is late this summer
135, line 35	tanku	tanka

SONIA SANCHEZ

THE BREATH/BREADTH
OF THE ANCESTORS

Several studies document the fairly familiar biograph-
ical information on Sonia Sanchez. Kalamu ya
Salaam's entry in the *Dictionary of Literary Biography* Vol. 41,
the interviews with Sanchez in D. H. Melhem's *Heroism in
the New Black Poetry: Introductions & Interviews*, Joanne
Braxton and Andree Nicola McLaughlin's *Wild Women in
the Whirlwind: Afra-American Culture and the Contemporary
Literary Renaissance*, and Claudia Tate's *Black Women Writers
at Work*—all provide information on Sanchez' life and the
interconnections between her life and her art.

Frenzella Elaine De Lancey's essay "This is Not a
Small Voice: Sonia Sanchez...Riddle for the Critics?" in *B.
Ma: The Sonia Sanchez Literary Review*, founded and edited
by De Lancey, provides the most up-to-date overview of
criticism on Sanchez. De Lancey addresses the stereotypical "reductionist" approaches to Sanchez' early poetry and
highlights the need for more comprehensive analyses of
her poetry. *B. Ma* (an acronym for Big Mama) is intended
as a contribution toward this endeavor. Published twice a
year, it has a challenging three-prong purpose: "to provide
an interdisciplinary forum for critical discussion of Sonia
Sanchez and other creative artists associated with the Black
Arts Movement and their organic connections with the
works of other Africans,...to promote contextualization of

the period,...to disseminate new knowledge about this important period of African American literary history; therefore, comparative studies of the works of Sonia Sanchez, other African American artists and other African artists will be given priority" (n. p.). While poet Sterling Plumpp is certainly astute when he says that the critics' and reviewers' neglect of much of the Black poetry that was written in the 1960s and 1970s, and of contemporary Black poetry as well, allows the poets to write and to express themselves without obstruction (Telephone conversation, 12 Aug. 1996), this critical dearth presents a void for literary history. Not only do we need individual studies of Sanchez', Plumpp's, Jayne Cortez', Eugene Redmond's, Haki Madhubuti's, Quincey Troupe's, Amiri Baraka's, Mari Evans', and Askia Toure's poetry, we also need studies that address the interrelationships and differences among these artists' works and philosophies. For example, while Sanchez, Madhubuti, and Baraka privilege jazz as a source of inspiration for their art, Plumpp grounds his poetry in a blues aesthetic and stresses the inextricable relationship between blues and jazz. *B. Ma* can become an essential forum for clearing up misconceptions, filling voids, and charting the direction of African-American poetry.

In addition to my earlier work on Sanchez (cited in the Preface), the most sustained critical analyses of Sanchez' poetry are De Lancey's above mentioned essay, Kalamu ya Salaam's bio-critical essay, and Houston A. Baker Jr.'s "Our Lady: Sonia Sanchez and the Writing of a Black Renaissance." Appreciating the interrelationship between Sanchez' poetry and her political and educational activities, Salaam provides a comprehensive analysis of her poetry from *Home Coming* (1969) to *homegirls & handgrenades* (1984). While Salaam identifies with Sanchez' connection between art and politics and with her work in establishing this connection as essential to the development of African-American Studies as a college discipline, Houston Baker emerges as quite ambivalent in his analysis of her poetry. Although his comparison of Sanchez to Black women blues artists and his explanation of Sanchez' and the blues women's connection with a nonelitist audience is useful, Baker avoids important issues in his comparison of the 1960s renaissance with the Harlem Renaissance.

Baker asserts that Alain Locke and others involved in the Harlem Renaissance were not really connected to the people; they, therefore, did not know or understand the possibilities the blues offered them. Thus, because of the nonelitist aspects of their poetry, Sanchez and others of the Black Arts Movement, according to Baker, are able to affect an audience in ways alien to Locke and his contemporaries (322-324). However Baker's language and a salient characteristic of all Sanchez' poetry that he ignores identify him with Alain Locke rather than with Sanchez, about whom Baker writes. Baker focuses heavily on the womanist nature of Sanchez' poetry, thus emphasizing Sanchez' early severe criticism of Black men who form intimate unions with White women. He gives only cursory attention to her more overtly political poems, such as "Malcolm" and "MIA's." When he does mention these poems and others, such as "Norma" and "Bubba," he focuses on those issues that reflect Sanchez' personal development rather than those that address her serious castigation of racism in its many guises. This stratagem and Baker's obfuscating language make his essay somewhat contradictory and suggest that as much distance exists between Baker and Sanchez as existed between Alain Locke and Langston Hughes.

In describing Sanchez as the Billie Holiday or Mamie Smith of the 1970s Black poetry arena, Baker places the Black linguistic concept of sounding at the center of his discussion. Henry Louis Gates Jr. in *The Signifying Monkey: A Theory of Afro-American Literary Criticism*, Geneva Smitherman in *Talkin and Testifyin: The Language of Black America*, and Carol D. Lee in *Signifying as a Scaffold for*

Literary Interpretation: The Pedagogical Implications of an African American Discourse Genre all indicate that sounding and the dozens are subcategories of signifying. Yet, Baker does not clarify for the reader his particular use of sounding. In his first use of the term in his essay on Sanchez, in reference to Alain Locke and his cohorts, Baker writes, "Rather than getting down with the folk, they valorized the folk from academic studies and editorial offices, only suggesting black national possibilities—rarely sounding them" (322). Baker's neglect to define or explain how this concept relates to his analogy between the levels of sounds (the music) and signifying (the Black figurative language of blues and jazz) in Billie Holiday's music and the levels of sounds (the rhythm) and signifying (the figurative Black speech) in Sanchez' poetry suggests that his essay is addressed to a rather limited audience. Although signifying inherently forbids the signifier to explain his or her meaning, as critic, Baker has the responsibility to ensure that his readers have all the information necessary to understand his codes. He falls prey to the same "bourgeois orientation," which he says stifled the success of the Harlem Renaissance.

According to Carol D. Lee, the readers of Baker's essay must question whether signifying works as well for the African-American literary critic as it does for the Black creative writer. She explains that Alain Locke and others of the Harlem Renaissance never resolved the tension between embracing a Black cultural ethos and using the structure of the White literary establishment whose fundamental assumption was that no connection exists between art and the masses (Telephone conversation, 17 Aug. 1996). Baker has the same problem. As he writes on a poet like Sonia Sanchez who, as others in the Black Arts Movement, honed her poetry for a large Black audience, he addresses a rather small audience, who may or may not understand that in sounding, the second participant must pick up the metaphor given by the first participant and turn that metaphor around in a creative way. To understand Baker's "Our Lady: Sonia Sanchez and the Writing of a Black Renaissance," the reader must also be technically familiar (must have more than cultural language acquisition) with the interrelationship among sounds, images, and rhythm in sounding and signifying because of the many assumptions that Baker makes.

One final quotation from Baker's essay focuses the points addressed above and demonstrates that Baker's condescending attitude toward the Black Arts Movement cannot be separated from his ambivalence in describing the nature of Sanchez' art, particularly since she was a key figure in this movement. Baker observes:

> What was absent in the hermeneutical moment of the sixties and seventies, however, was a distinctive Afro-American critical and creative vocabulary predicated upon authentic *sounds* (say, blues sounds) of our national life. What we witnessed, therefore, was black nationalist political scientists, literary critics, theologians, and political activists submitting—time and again—analyses that read and resonated to the rhythms and tonalities of a white American groove. For example, rather than rejecting out of hand the entire discursive field surrounding a deeply class-invented word like "aesthetic," black literary critics and *artists* [emphasis mine] merely readopted this field, proclaiming themselves *black aestheticians* (325).

While poet and critic Lorenzo Thomas is certainly astute in pointing out that the Black Arts Movement technically refers to many of the Black creative writers on the scene in the 1970s and that the Black aestheticians were critics, such as Addison Gayle, Hoyt Fuller, and Stephen Henderson, who were trained literary critics (The MLA

Convention 1995), it is also true that many of the then young writers of the Black Arts Movement, such as Amiri Baraka, Larry Neal, Sonia Sanchez, Haki Madhubuti, and Sarah Fabio, also published literary criticism that posited their own Black aesthetic perspectives. Consequently, in the above passage, Baker must include Sanchez in his list of "black nationalist political scientists" who hypocritically contradicted themselves by "creating a vocabulary predicated upon authentic *sounds*...of our national life" and by calling this creation a Black aesthetic.

As the following essays on the history of African-American poetry and on Sanchez' entire poetic canon to date demonstrate, African-American poetry, though written in English, has always reflected a cultural particularity that distinguishes it from Euro-American poetry. Sonia Sanchez and her peers, who began publishing poetry in the late 1960s, challenged the elitism of Eurocentric poetry both stylistically and philosophically. To denounce these poets (and their peer critics) for using a Eurocentric term to describe their methodology emerges as merely a means of avoiding discussion on those characteristics of their art that are creatively and politically nontraditional. An element of this avoidance is Baker's isolating Sanchez, his failure to place her in context or among her peers, such as Baraka, Madhubuti, Neal, or Toure. By neglecting to show that Sanchez is part of a larger movement, Baker downplays the power of the movement.

The essays "Bantu, Nkodi, Ndungu, and Nganga" and "The Continuing Journey of Sonia Sanchez: from *homegirls & handgrenades* to *Wounded in the House of a Friend*" exemplify the goal of this book to reject the "discursive field surrounding a deeply class-invested" (to use Baker's words) Eurocentric approach to African-American poetry. What I attempt to show in this study is that the theoretical foundations of African-American poetry are of African origin and that Sonia Sanchez' stylistic development moves progressively back toward her African roots. In other words, she began to form the substantial African characteristics of her current poetry in the late 1960s and early 1970s. Analogously, Sanchez' poetry, her two essays in *Crisis and Culture*, the poetry and essays of her peers and the critical contributions of Hoyt Fuller, Addison Gayle, and especially Stephen Henderson are the foundations on which this study is based. *Ijala: Sonia Sanchez and the African Poetic Tradition* then is a continuation of the Black Arts Movement. By using African terminology for a theoretical foundation for the history of African-American poetry and by grounding Sanchez' poetry in an African tradition, this study continues the work Stephen Henderson began in *Understanding the New Black Poetry*, whereby a critical paradigm grows out of Sanchez' poetry rather than imposing one on it.

Like Sanchez' poetry, this study attempts to be accessible to diverse readers, both trained and untrained in reading literary criticism. In the same way that Sanchez identifies with her audience, the aim of this study is to destroy elitism and distance and thus resolve that tension that Carol D. Lee and Houston Baker describe in Alain Locke and his contemporaries. Baker himself is unable to resolve this tension and becomes entrapped by it because of his avoidance of Sanchez' unequivocal and unapologetic attack on the evils of racism. This attack, moreover, is rooted in Sanchez' sounding: her ingenious ability to pick up the insults and abuses of racism and turn them around in a creative and provocative way. The success of Sanchez' sounding rests on the peculiar ways in which she manipulates the establishment's poetic language and reshapes it to satisfy her African poetics. While Sanchez' most stylistically innovative poems best reflect her creative genius, Baker and others refer to these poems, such as "to Chuck," as "experimental" (335), suggesting that the form of this poem is inferior to those poems that follow the tradition of poetry supported by the Eurocentric literary establishment.

Sanchez' explanation as to why she writes and her comments on her obsession with revisions of her poetry indirectly respond to critics, such as Baker and Roderick Palmer, an early reviewer, who position themselves outside of the tradition to which Sanchez belongs and who undermine her creative genius. In her interview with Claudia Tate in the early 1980s, Sanchez makes it clear that she repeatedly revises her poetry. When Tate asks Sanchez how she fits writing into her life, Sanchez responds:

> One year I taught five courses and finished two books. I work from midnight to around three every morning on my writing...At a quarter to twelve all that stops [attention to children, grading papers, and answering letters]. Then my writing starts...I work in two or three notebooks; I still have all the notebooks from the ten books I've done. I do everything long-hand. I hate to see first drafts. I read them out loud. They're terrible, and then I read successive drafts...Then the final draft...all the steps cannot be seen in the draft" (141-42).

Clearly, Sanchez regards her poetry as artistic contributions that surpass the level of experimentation. For inherent in the word *experimental* is the negative connotation that a poem is inferior in some way. Thus this term is often used by those who hold elitist concepts rooted in a Eurocentric poetic tradition to describe the typographical and rhythmic innovations of the Black Arts writers.

Sanchez' comments on how she writes and those on why she writes demonstrate that she takes for granted the idea that poetry can be both political and artistically well crafted. During the early 1980s in Mari Evans' *Black Women Writers*, Sanchez explains:

> To answer the question of how I write, we must

> look also to why I write. I write to tell the truth
> about the Black condition as I see it. Therefore I
> write to offer a Black woman's view of the
> world. How I tell the truth is part of the truth
> itself. I've always believed that the truth con-
> cealed or clouded is a partial lie. So when I
> decide to tell the truth about an event/happen-
> ing. It must be clear and understandable for
> those who need to understand the lie/lies being
> told. What I learned in deciding "how" to write
> was simply that most folks tend to think that
> you're lying or jiving them if you have to spice
> things up just to get a point across (415-16).

These comments recall Sanchez' listing of the six characteristics of African liberation poetry in *Crisis and Culture* discussed above.

Sanchez places herself within the African tradition, in
which art, in this case poetry, was closely connected to the
quality of the people's lives, and the artist, priest, or performer enjoyed the responsibility of educating and inspiring his/her people. She says, "Like the priest and the
prophet, with whom he/she was often *synonymous*, the
poet in some societies has had infinite powers to interpret
life; in others his/her voice has been drowned out by the
winds of mundane pursuits" (*Black Women Writers* 417).
Sanchez refers here to the same tradition Isidore Okpewho
describes in *African Oral Literature: Backgrounds, Character,
and Continuity*. In explaining that African oral literature
grows out of its people's lives, Okpewho says, "A much
wider service provided by oral literature is to give the society—whether isolated groups within it or the citizenry as a
whole—a collective sense of who they are and to help them
define or comprehend the world at large in terms both
familiar and positive to them" (110). Not only does
Sanchez adopt the same purpose for her art as the African-
oral performer, she also began to appropriate some of the

themes of African poetry early in her career.

In addition to referring to the political content of the East African Islamic poets in *Crisis and Culture*, Sanchez also began to use the form of this Swahili poetry to shape her own poetry. In her interview with D. H. Melhem, she cites Swahili praise poetry as a significant influence on her book-length autobiographical poem *Blues Book for Blue Black Magical Women* (*Heroism* 165). Again, when I wrote the essay "The Development of Sonia Sanchez: A Continuing Journey" included here, I was not aware of the specific influences of African poetry on Sanchez' art. These influences became increasingly obvious to me over the years and were confirmed by my discovery of Isidore Okpewho's *African Oral Literature*. In a recent discussion with the poet, Sanchez provides details and background to illustrate how *Blues Book* emerges as the foundation of the stylistic strength of her current poetry.

She explains that she had begun writing *Blues Book* while teaching at a New York community college. The book derives from the image of a female African ancestor that came to the poet in a dream during a very difficult time in the poet's life when she was "whiteballed" for having participated in a strike with students over the development of an African-American Studies Department. At the time, Sanchez was a member of the Nation of Islam and was well-versed in the teachings of the Honorable Elijah Muhammed. She was also reading the literature of the Sub-Saharan civilizations of West and East Africa and the *Egyptian Book of the Dead*. (Telephone interview, 24 Aug. 1996). Sanchez was significantly influenced by the praise poetry that characterizes Swahili oral literature. She conceived *Blues Book* as a series of praise songs to the mother, father, and the self. These poems, she says, "fix you into what you should be." Although the book is autobiographical, she uses the self as representative of a larger self. She celebrates people's achievement. Thus the book is a "rallying point for present-day people" (Telephone Interview, August 24, 1996).

Isidore Okpewho 's description of praise poetry places this verse in a political tradition and thereby explains Sanchez' comprehensive use of it in her verse. In his discussion of the training of the poet for *ifa* divination and of the *ijala* poet, Okpewho explains that "the issues of training and patronage are closely connected because, in many ways, the type of oral literature that the artist trains for depends on the kinds of people who listen to him" (25). He divides patronage into two broad categories: public and private. Poets who praise the king, his family background, the greatness of his family, as well as the king's personal attributes and accomplishments receive private patronage. "Besides private patronage offered by the royal court, there is what may be seen as the semi-private patronage offered by distinguished individuals in a community, like a warrior, a hunter, or a politician (Okpewho 27). In addition to these court or royal artists, African oral literature and history include the occasional poetry of griots who perform at weddings, funerals, and other celebrations or ceremonies (Okpewho 28).

Extending the parameters or focus of the praise poem, Sanchez transforms the traditional praise poem into a form that politicizes the realities of Black people's lives in America. Understanding well the tradition out of which she writes, she establishes the connection between love and praise that Okpewho makes. While Sanchez says that love and praise are related (Telephone Interview, 24 Aug. 1996), Okpewho writes, "The theme of praise is to a certain extent similar to that of love, for both sentiments are fundamentally based in a feeling of admiration for a person or an object" (142). Sanchez and Okpewho both affirm the hyperbolic nature of praise poetry. While Sanchez says that *Blues Book* suggests possibilities that are bigger than life (Telephone Interview), Okpewho says that "the language of praise is usually lofty and exaggerated....[T]he poet must show in what way that subject qualifies for the attention above anyone else. Consequently, in praise poetry we often find the subject given attributes and characteristics that are either not possible within the laws of nature or at least go somewhat beyond the truth" (142-43). The lines "this woman, wet with wandering/reviving the beauty of forests and winds" from *Blues Book* are an example of such exaggeration. In a poem such as *Blues Book*, in which the poet uses her life and African origins to inspire other Black women to affirm their African identity and seek the best within themselves, Sanchez exaggerates to emphasize the uniqueness of the African-American woman. Thus Sanchez' praise poetry emerges out of a tradition in which the griots/poets, functioning as guides, teachers, and historians for their respective cultures, embrace their people.

Despite the communal and political nature of African oral poetry, technical skill was an important requirement for the oral performer. Okpewho observes that "whatever the environment in which artists find themselves, all of them are trained in fundamentally the same skills: the sensitive use of words and images, the delicate balance between music and words, the art of holding the attention or interest of an audience" (29). In discussing the technical attention she gave to *Blues Book*, Sanchez says, "I am always enamored of the craft of poetry. When you get lost in that craft or form, you come out smiling. It's like that first moment of making love. It's the same kind of thing as being in the classroom and making a point and seeing the students get it. It's that kind of joy" (Telephone interview, 24 Aug. 1996).

East African Islamic poetry in Swahili has also significantly influenced Sanchez' *Blues Book*. The poets privileged form over content: "Almost all Swahili prosodic terms refer to form. Themes are important but they are regarded as potentially known in a closed society....The merit of a poet

therefore would rest largely on his choice of words and the
way he combines them, that is his use of syntax and also on
his ability to create fresh idiom and metaphor and to use
the existing ones in unexpected yet striking contexts"
(Abdulaziz 66). Sanchez' poetry abounds with such fresh
and striking images as "sitting still in domestic bacteria,"
"rap your feet around justice," "and gangster shadows."
The appearance of *Blues Book*, moreover, reveals a marked
change in the style of her poetry. While both *Home Coming*
(1969) and *We a BaddDDD People* (1970) are artistically well-
honed, they lack the lyrical and contemplative nature of
African praise poetry that appears first in *Blues Book* and
continues in Sanchez' current works.

Although Sanchez' early critics and reviewers, such as
George Kent and R. Roderick Palmer, pay serious attention
to her style, neither of them makes a connection between
the simplicity of her language, the extension of word
sounds, and the use of abbreviated words (Kent 198;
Palmer 36) with the African oral tradition. In discussing
Muyaka bin Haji's Swahili poetry, Mohamed Abdulaziz
states the same characteristics of this poetry that Kent cites
for Sanchez, but, more importantly, Abdulaziz' descrip-
tions coincide with the key terms Stephen Henderson uses
to describe the new Black poetry of the 1960s. The characteristics Abdulaziz attributes to East African poetry—allusions, compressed style, balanced style, emphasizing
words by repeating them, alliterations, and play on words
(90-97)—all correspond to Henderson's virtuoso naming
and enumerating (repetition), jazzy rhythmic effect (alliteration and repetition), virtuoso free-rhyming (word play),
hyperbolic imagery (exaggeration/play on words), understatement (compressed style), and compressed and cryptic
imagery (compressed style). In tracing the salient characteristics of Black poetry of the 1960s back to the "forms of
things unknown" in the Black folk slave community,
Henderson stops one step short of demonstrating the pres-

ence of African verbal art in a community that logically would have manifested an African verbal presence despite the irreversible intrusion of English. Although retention of African linguistic forms by the slaves and their descendants seems to have been unconscious, Sanchez' use of such forms are quite deliberate. "A Poem of Praise (for Gerald Penny. . .)" and "Kwa mama zetu waliotuzaa" collected in *I've Been a Woman: New and Selected Poems* (1978); "Reflections After the June 12th March for Disarmament" in *homegirls and handgrenades* (1984); "shigeko: a hiroshima maiden speaks," "3 x 3 Carl: a Black man Speaks," and "the poet: speaks after silence" in *Under a Soprano Sky* (1987); and "Improvisation" in *Wounded in the House of a Friend* (1995) are all praise poems. It is significant that traditional Swahili praise poetry lost much of its rhythm, meter, and rhyme on translation into English. Although Sanchez does not restore the rhyme to this poetry, she does depend heavily upon repetition to achieve rhythm.

Although Sanchez cites Alexander Pushkin and Federico Garcia Lorca (152) as influences on her early poetry in her interview with D. H. Melhem, the influence of the African tradition emerges as the most sustained. Although Pushkin's poetry took diverse forms, including lyrical poems, dramas, narrative poems, verse novels, and tales in verse, his exact influence on Sanchez' craft is somewhat difficult to discern. Sanchez' eight collections of adult poetry are distinctly different from each other. They demonstrate the experiential and intellectual growth she brings to her art. This diversity, perhaps, emerges as her strongest connection with Pushkin. However, the intensely lyrical and imagistic quality of *Under a Soprano Sky* suggests an ongoing influence of Lorca on her poetry. The most lyrical and enigmatic of all her collections, *Under a Soprano Sky* contains similar natural images that challenge our imagination, such as these lines from Federico Garcia Lorca's poetry: "His heart was growing full/of broken wings and rag flowers" (161) or "The world was left behind/a lily of cotton and shadow" (147).

These lines from Lorca indirectly challenge the idea that Sanchez is basically a woman's poet. Not only is her lyrical language not exclusively female-identified but the issues she addresses affect the lives of men and women individually and collectively. The argument that Sanchez is a woman's poet has the same stereotypical and inherent contradiction as the idea that Black literature that depicts racism is not universal. Just as Black literature that addresses racism connects Black and White people as well as people of color, Sanchez' poetry that challenges the evils of Black-male sexism has men as part of the subject, and thus their role in Sanchez' poetry is as essential as the role of Whites in African-American literature. From *Home Coming* to *Wounded in the House of a Friend*, Sanchez has consistently stressed the need for Black men to reevaluate their self-concept and the impact that their self-concept has on their relationship with Black women. Poems such as "to all brothers" and "to a jealous cat" from *Home Coming*; "poem for etheridge" in *We a BaddDDD People*; "To You/Who Almost Turned/Me On" from *Love Poems*; "Just Don't Never Give Up on Love" and "To All Brothers: From All Sisters" from *homegirls & handgrenades*; "3 x 3 Carl: a Black man Speaks" in *Under a Soprano Sky*; and "Wounded in the House of a Friend" and "Eyewitness: Case No. 3456" from *Wounded in the House of a Friend*; as well as numerous haiku and tanka poems all invite Black men to examine an aspect of their psyches which allow them to ignore, exploit, hate, rape, beat, and generally harass Black women.

Channeling her personal experiences through her imagination, Sanchez avoids hostility and self-pity in these poems that seek to affect Black men. Critic Lauren Francis recognizes that Sanchez assesses Black women as critically as she admonishes Black men: "Existence-in-relationship is an important aspect of Sonia Sanchez' poetry. Her poetic illustrations of fear, struggle and love from the Black woman's perspective are balanced with a complementarity which focuses on the fear, oppression and anger of Black men....Sanchez not only hears the Black man, [*sic*] she provides forum and possible audience via her poems. This then characterizes Sanchez as an Afrocentric womanist. Her compassion runs so deep and so true, that she is able to offer herself as medium through which African American men may speak" (54 and 59). The poems "Wounded in the House of a Friend" and "Eyewitness: Case No. 3456" from the poet's most recent collection emerge as the most complex of all such poems throughout her canon in which she speaks to and for Black men.

Both of these poems embody at least three voices—the poet's, the men's, and the reader's perception of the poet's critique of Black male behavior. These triple-voiced poems present intriguing challenges to those scholars interested in the application of what Mikhail Bahktin refers to as *heteroglossia*, the idea that meaning depends on the circumstances that evoke the uttering of a word. However, for our purposes, what is most important is Sanchez' purpose in having Black males speak through her, or in her adopting their voices. Because "Eyewitness: Case No. 3455" presents a vivid and sustained description of a man raping a woman, it ruptures our emotions more severely than "Wounded in the House of a Friend," although this poem is quite powerful as well. When asked to respond to the background or inspiration for "Eyewitness," Sanchez explains that she took the language in the poem from South African women's recordings of their harassment and oppression. She says that she wanted the readers to see the perpetrator, and she wanted men to understand what happens and hear themselves raping a women. She wanted to keep men from objectifying rape (Telephone interview, 30 Mar. 1996).

Sanchez' comments on the purpose of her poem recalls the definition of poetry that appears in her work as early as 1983: "...poetry is a subconscious conversation, it is as much the work of those who understand it and those who make it" (*Crisis and Culture* 2). Sanchez then is optimistic that a bond connects her to the Black men who read her poetry and who hear her read it. This racial bond finds its roots in an African heritage and in African-Americans' shared history of slavery. The bond, however, does not exclude other people of color, Europeans, and Euro-Americans. In an interview with Claudia Tate, Sanchez is very clear and specific in her answer to Tate's question "For whom do you write?":

> I write. . . because I think one must not only share what one thinks, or the conclusions one has reached, but one must also share to help others reach their conclusions. Writing might help them survive. My audience has always been a black audience. But I have also found that other people have picked up on my writing. Therefore, I might say that I write for progressive people. My work has been translated into European languages. White people write to me about my work, and say that I have touched them, that it's been painful, but it's made them grow. I've always known I have whites in my audience. America has tried to say that that's not true and has tried to isolate people. (142)

Significantly, Sanchez begins her response to Tate's question by clarifying why she writes; thus why she writes is inextricably related to the audience she addresses. It is also clear that Sanchez' perspective would challenge Jacques Derrida's notion of freeplay or decentering. Clearly, she believes in a stable point of reference that unites poet, message, and audience. At the same time,

Sanchez and others of the Black Arts Movement believe that the text is related to a reality outside itself; they also, as she makes clear above, believe that texts cannot be objective and that this requirement of objectivity has always been a ruse the White intellectual elite uses to serve its own purposes. However, the ideas of Sanchez and others of the Black Arts Movement, such as Haki Madhubuti, Amiri Baraka, Larry Neal, and Sarah Webster Fabio, have so far not been compared with those European or Euro-American reader-response critics, such as George Poulet, Michael Riffaterre, Wolfgang Iser, Stanley Fish, and Jane Tompkins, who all, to varying degrees, deny the existence of objective texts. When Sanchez identifies her audience as multicultural and her Black subjects or issues as universal, she strikes at the core of the problem of objectivity.

Human beings unite or connect around various issues according to how their experiences reflect their cultural backgrounds, social level or class, political ideology, religious belief, education, integrity, and emotional depth. Every work of art then reflects some combination of these factors as well as others, and each work challenges the reader's ability to identify in some way with the issues presented. Appreciation of a particular work of art comes by means of identification. Consequently, rather than demanding objectivity from its creative artists, literary critics, and theorists, the western literary tradition should stress the values and limitations of *identification*. For when Sanchez says that she writes in order to help people survive, she is acknowledging that the combination of the writer's skill in expressing his/her vision and the reader's ability to connect or identify with that vision is a great source of power. This power has been stifled historically by the western literary elite, which predates and includes the new critics, and by the post-structuralists who followed them. Both post-structuralists and new critics share the idea that texts are not responsible for reality. Yet, Sanchez and Haki Madhubuti, who writes , "Black writers...deal in images. They understand the uses and manipulation of the image" (96), clearly defy the western tradition in their notion that discourse/art *is* responsible for reality.

Nothing demonstrates the power of discourse to change reality more than the examples of two lives that have been changed or have taken an alternative course because of Sanchez' oral and written poetic performances. Perhaps the best example of discourse creating reality is the fact that most professors' political and intellectual ideologies as well as their linguistic methodologies are direct results of the training they receive in graduate school. When I graduated from the University of Georgia in 1979, I would have continued to explore texts through new critical lenses if I had not discovered the poetry, essays, and performances of Sonia Sanchez. Preparation for writing on her poetry required my exploring the history of and works by other writers of the Black Arts Movement. *Identifying* with the ideas presented by these writers directly led to the perspective I took in the 1987 publication of my essay "The Black Canon: Reconstructing Black American Literary Criticism." This essay provoked responses by Houston A. Baker Jr. and Henry Louis Gates Jr. which in turn, led to my current position outside the mainstream of African-American literary criticism, because its leading figures follow the ideology of the Euro-American theoretical and critical tradition.

The influence of Sonia Sanchez' and the Black Arts Movement's discourse on a younger generation is manifested most beautifully in the works of D-Knowledge, a twenty-five year-old performance poet with whom Sanchez performs a poem on D-Knowledge's 1995 album *All That and a Bag of Words*. A Ph. D. candidate in sociology at the University of California, Los Angeles, D-Knowledge fuses his academic training with his knowledge of Black history and his skill in writing Black poetry.

Upon listening to or reading his poetry for the first time, we hear the voices of Sonia Sanchez, Amiri Baraka, Carolyn Rodgers, Askia Toure, and Haki Madhubuti. Like these writers, D-Knowledge roots his poetry in the diversified heritage of Black music, in rhythm and blues, blues, jazz, and gospel.   His advice to young Black men who abuse themselves and Black women by assuming their mack-daddy persona demonstrates that, like Sanchez, his language is rooted in the Black speech of his contemporaries. Following Sanchez and the African poetic tradition, D-Knowledge, in his own words, "take(s) words that mean one thing and turn them around so that they mean another."

Sanchez and D-Knowledge's reading/performance of her poem "Catch the Fire," which appears in *Wounded in the House of Friend*, demonstrates how discourse influences and changes reality. Reminiscent of the poetry perfor-mance that took place in nightclubs, on street corners, and in parks in the late 1960s and early 1970s, the sound track from this song and others appear to have been recorded in a nightclub with an audience whose applause and affirma-tion play a role in the performance. A saxophone solo plays throughout the performance of the poem, comple-menting and responding to both Sanchez and D-Knowledge. At different moments, the saxophone speaks to them, simultaneously or separately. Demonstrating the complementarity and the need for bonding between the Black man and woman, Sanchez and D-Knowledge speak to each other, reciting lines alternately and complementing each other in much the same way as the sun and the moon in Sanchez' *Blues Book for Blue Black Magical Women*. The fire that they ask the Black man and women to catch is the fire of knowledge, strength, endurance, creativity, and courage that sustain Black survival.

Sanchez' performance on D-Knowledge's album reflects her awareness of the role the recording industry plays in affecting the lives of Black people. In 1983, she observes:

> The poet as lyricist may well occupy center stage in the 1980s. In the 1980s, Black value setting may well be a struggle between subliminal seduction of Black moral strength presented by poetic lyrics of songs: *Disco Lady, Le Freak,...Breaking the Funk*, ad nauseam, and a new movement to instill positive Black family and social values. Nowhere in the annals of man's hypnotism or suggestology has such a massive undermining of the moral fabric of a people been so undertaken as in today's music industry. Record lyrics, through repetition and rhythm, are producing behavior which is contrary to human development and self-contemplation, producing moral schizophrenics and escapism through drugs...Poets need to become moral psychologists in the 1980s. (*Crisis and Culture* 14)

Thus, in performing with D-Knowledge, Sanchez attempts to extend her audience to the younger generation, who fanatically buys tapes and CDs, but who may never have heard of her poetry. She and others of the Black Arts Movement—specifically Askia Toure, Haki Madhubuti, Amiri Baraka, and Nikki Giovanni—have all recorded their poetry to music, attempting to reach the large audience which is often manipulated by the escape-from-reality and get-rich-quickly schemes of the record industry. In functioning as moral psychologists, Sanchez also performs a poem with the noted, Washington, DC based, female acappella group Sweet Honey and the Rock. The song and poem "Stay on the Battlefield" appears on the group's most recent recording *Sacred Ground* (1995). A praise poem aimed at inspiring Black people to celebrate the strength, endurance, and struggle that characterize Black survival, "Stay on the Battlefield" is a freedom song, which Sanchez

recites as the group sings in the melody of a Black spiritual. Because the Black spiritual represents the strongest of
the African-American's survival traditions, the poem
emerges as a fight for liberation in which the battlefield is
life itself. Sweet Honey in the Rock's and D-Knowledge's
recordings offer alternatives to the proliferation of hip-hop
music in today's market. Although most rap music demonstrates that today's younger generation is far more politically astute than their parents were when young some rap
music, particularly gangster rap, reflects the "hypnotic
behavior which is contrary to human development"
Sanchez addresses.

Having recited her poems on at least six recordings of
her own between 1968 and 1982, Sanchez remains persistent in her continuing journey to extend the range of her
audience. Regardless of the medium, she emerges as an
African poet who places concern for the quality of her people's lives at the center of her artistry. Her travels to Cuba,
Nicaragua, China, Norway, England, Australia, the
Caribbean, and Africa suggest the multicultural/interna-
tional perspective of her art. Her performance at the 1996
Black Arts Festival in Atlanta reflects her growth as an
artist and captures her performance as an African oral performer. A member of the panel "My Dungeon Shook: The
Language of Resistance in African-American Literary
Traditions" with Amiri Baraka, Mari Evans, and Haki
Madhubuti, Sanchez ignored the written text she had
before her when her time came to speak. Instead of reading what she had written, she stood up and began to
address the audience extemporaneously, totally inspired
by the subject, the faces, and responses of the audience.
She captivated the audience by challenging it to *resist* all
actions and ideologies that stifle human development and
by challenging it to become active rather than following a
trend toward passivity that characterizes the 1990s. In the
call-and-response tradition, she began a chant in which she

asked the audience a question and it responded by reciting
resist as loudly as it could. Sanchez appeared to be in a
trance, her face reflecting pain and sorrow, as she discussed
the dilemmas that confront Blacks all over the world. She
clearly transfixed and transformed the audience. Her success with this technique has its roots in an African oral tradition in which the words of the artist become an integral
part of the artist's entire deportment. Isidore Okpewho
explains the interconnectedness between the literary and
the extraliterary in the African oral tradition:

> But oral artists use more than their mouths to
> express their words; to consider the effectiveness
> of the words, therefore, we should examine the
> usefulness of those accompanying resources
> where such information is available or can be
> deduced. These accompanying resources are
> variously described as nonverbal, extraverbal,
> paraverbal, paratextual, or paralinguistic, in the
> sense that they occur side by side with the text or
> the words of literature. One of these resources is
> the histrionics of the performance, that is, move-
> ments made with the face, hands, or any other
> part of the body as a way of dramatically
> demonstrating an action contained in the text.
> (46)

As demonstrated by her performance at the Black Arts
Festival, Sanchez plants her literary roots in an African tradition, a tradition which requires her to communicate effec-
tively with, challenge, educate, and enliven her people. In
fulfilling her task, she has not only been inspired to move
beyond her text, she has been consistent in addressing the
contemporary themes or issues that have affected Black
people for the past three decades.

The next chapter places Sanchez within the context of
the entire African-American poetic tradition, while chap-

ters three and four focus specifically on the development
of her poetry. They demonstrate that her themes reflect the
diverse political problems Blacks have faced in Africa, the
Caribbean, and the United States. In this poetry we see the
particular manifestation of *bantu, nkodi, ndungu, and nganga*
in African-American poetry.

WORKS CITED

Abdulaziz, Mohamed H. Muyaka: *19th Century Swahili Popular Poetry.* Nairobi: Kenya Literature Bureau, 1979.

Baker Jr., Houston A. "Our Lady: Sonia Sanchez and the Writing of a Black Renaissance." In *Reading Black, Reading Feminist: A Critical Anthology.* Ed. Henry Louis Gates Jr. NY: Meridian, 1990. 318-47.

De Lancey, Frenzella Elaine. "This is Not a Small Voice: Sonia Sanchez...Riddle for the Critics?" *B. Ma: The Sonia Sanchez Review* 1 (1995): 30-51.

Francis, Lauren. "Sonia Sanchez's Common Cause: Grounding with the Brothers." *B. Ma: The Sonia Sanchez Literary Review* 1 (1995): 52-65.

Lorca, Federico Garcia. "Suicide." Trans. Jerome Rothenberg. *Federico Garcia Lorca: Selected Verse.* Ed. Christopher Maurer. NY: Farrar Strauss Giroux, 1995. 161.

Madhubuti, Haki R. *From Plan to Planet.* Chicago: Third World Press, 1973.

Okpewho, Isidore. *African Oral Literature: Backgrounds, Character, and Continuity.* Bloomington: Indiana U P, 1992.

Sanchez, Sonia. *Crisis and Culture: Two Speeches by Sonia Sanchez.* NY: Black Liberation Press, 1983.

_____. "Ruminations/Reflections." In *Black Women Writers (1950-1980): A Critical Evaluation*. Ed. Mari Evans. NY: Anchor/Doubleday, 1984. 415-18.

_____. "Sonia Sanchez: The Will and the Spirit." In *Heroism in the New Black Poetry: Introductions & Interviews*. Ed. D. H. Melhem. Lexington: U P of Kentucky, 1990. 133-79.

_____. "Interview." In *Black Women Writers at Work*. Ed. Claudia Tate. NY: Continuum, 1983. 132-48.

CHAPTER ONE

BANTU, NKODI, NDUNGU, AND NGANGA

LANGUAGE, POLITICS, MUSIC, & RELIGION IN AFRICAN AMERICAN POETRY

"Downpressor Man"

dooownpressor man
where you gonna run to

dooownpressor man
where you go to

dooownpressor man
where you gonna run to

allll along that day

you gonna run to the sea
but the sea will be boiling
when you run to the sea
the sea will be boiling
when you run to the sea
the sea will be boiling

allll along that day

you gonna run to the rocks
the rocks will be melting
when you run to the rocks
the rocks will be melting
when you run to the rocks

the rocks will be melting

I said allll along that day

so I said dooownpressor man
where you gonna run to
I SAID dooownpressor man
where you gonna run to
I said dooownpressor man
where you gonna run to

allll along that day

you drink your big champagne
and laugh

ha ha ha ha ha ha

you drink your big champagne
and laugh

ha ha ha ha ha ha ha ha

you drink your big champagne
and laugh

ha   ha

allll along that day

I wouldn't like to be a flea
under your collar   man

I wouldn't like to be a flea
under your collar   man

I wouldn't like to be a flea
on your collar

allll along that day

you can run
but you can't hide

you can run
but you can't hide

you can run
but you can't hide

telling you
allll along that day

you gonna run to the law
beggin 'im to hide you

you gonna run to the law
beggin 'im to hide you

you gonna run to Jah
beggin 'im to hide you

allll

allll

along that day

and I said dooownpressor man

where you gonna run to

where you gonna run to

dooownpressor man
where you gonna run to

I said

all along

along

that way

dooownpressor man
dooownpressor man
dooownpressor man
dooownpressor man

where

dooownpressor man

whereyougonnarunto

dooownpressor man

idonknowwhereyougonnarunto

all along that day

dooownpressor man

you can't run
you can't bribe Jah Jah

don't call 'im in a bar
he can drink some berry soup

don't bribe 'im
around the corner
don't tes 'im faith

dooownpressor man

lawd
dooownpressor man

I said dooownpressor man

don run

downpressor man
downpressor man

where you gonna run tooooooooooooo

dooownpressor man

you can't bribe no one
ther don want no money

they run fe money
cause money get funny

dooownpressor man

Peter Tosh

Peter Tosh's "Downpressor Man" serves as a paradigm for my exploration of the African-American
poetic tradition, a tradition with roots in Africa and flowers
that manifest throughout the diaspora. Tosh, one of the
greatest and most spiritual of the grassroots Reggae musicians, sings of oppression. The downpressor man is the
white man or white society and all of its unjust laws. Tosh,
a Rastafarian, believes that the Rastafarians are descendants of the tribe of Judah, one of the twelve tribes that
were saved in the Book of Revelations. Thus in his song,
the boiling sea and the melting rocks are allusions to the

great mountain burning with fire that an angel cast into the sea during the destruction of the earth in the eighth chapter of the Book of Revelations.

Tosh's song exists on two levels: while he sings of Armageddon and uses Biblical references, he also attacks racial oppression and presages the destruction of the power that Whites wield over Blacks. Addressing white society, or the downpressor man, Tosh warns that when the day comes for Blacks to take control of their lives, Whites will have to have a place to run to. They will not be able to hide, their laws will not protect them, and Jah (Yahweh) will not heed their begging. On this day of reckoning, the Black man or woman will not succumb to the lure of money because he or she will have finally realized that money gets funny. In other words, the monetary system is not based on the gold that is in the reserve, it is controlled by a private industry with arbitrary standards. At one time pennies were made of pure copper; now they are basically zinc and lead. And while the nickel was once made of silver, it is now made of an alloy. Thus, the White society's haughtiness, reflected in their laughing over their champagne, will dissipate on the great day of wrath when Blacks demand honor.

The process of transcribing Tosh's song reveals the linguistic, political, religious, and rhythmic features that link Black poetry in the diaspora. Following the tradition established by Black poets in the 1960s, I do not capitalize any of the words in Tosh's song. I also use very few commas and periods. Clearly, Tosh, like Sonia Sanchez and Haki Madhubuti, would express his rebellion against Eurocentric poetic form through the use of innovative typography and the absence of capitalization. I also had to make decisions about the typography of the poem, using Tosh's voice and the rhythm of his music as signs for which lines to write together and which to separate with spaces. I also use his voice as a guide for deciding how a word should be spelled. Therefore, I put three o's in *downpressor* and four *l*'s in *all* because of the way he extends these syllables as he sings. I use his voice as a signal not only for spelling and for spacing lines, but also for spacing words that I put on a single line. Sometimes I may put only one or two words on a single line, or I might compress eight words together.

In transcribing the song, I became acutely aware that the Black poetry of the 1960s had left an indelible and far-reaching influence on contemporary African-American poetry. However, the linguistic, political, musical, and religious features of Tosh's song informs the entire African-American poetic tradition from Phillis Wheatley, Jupiter Hammon, George Moses Horton, James Monroe Whitfield, Frances Ellen Watkins Harper, James Edwin Campbell, Paul Laurence Dunbar, Fenton Johnson, James Weldon Johnson, Jean Toomer, Claude McKay, Countee Cullen, Melvin B. Tolson, Georgia Douglas Johnson, Helene Johnson, Alice Dunbar Nelson, Angelina Grimke, Langston Hughes, Frank Marshall Davis, Waring Cuney, Sterling Brown, Owen Dodson, Gwendolyn Brooks, Margaret Walker, Robert Hayden, Pinkie Gordon Lane, Naomi Long Madgett, Mari Evans, Gloria Oden, Henry Dumas, Askia Toure, Etheridge Knight, Amiri Baraka, Sonia Sanchez, Haki Madhubuti, Audre Lorde, Jay Wright, Lucille Clifton, Jayne Cortez, Sterling Plumpp, Eugene Redmond, Michael Harper, June Jordan, Pat Parker, Al Young, Calvin Forbes, Nikki Giovanni, Angela Jackson, Marilyn Nelson Waniek, Rita Dove, Alexis de Veaux, Ntozake Shange, Essex Hemphill, Hattie Gossett, E. Ethelbert Miller, Quincy Troupe, Daryl Holmes, Elizabeth Alexander, Wanda Coleman, Michael Warr, Ruth Forman, Kevin Powell, Ras Baraka, to D-Knowledge.

This catalog is consciously overwhelming with the intention of underscoring the diversity, productivity, and richness of our poetic tradition and of presenting a historical pool of writers, most of whose works (with amazingly few exceptions) to varying degrees and in varying ways reflect the interconnection of language, politics, music, and religion in African-American poetry. This interconnection is clearly obvious in the works of the young writers whose poems appear in *In the Tradition: An Anthology of Young Black Writers*, edited by Kevin Powell and Ras Baraka (1992). I would like to suggest that any theory of African-American poetry must place these four features at the center of its exposition.

In the totally engaging study *A Profile of Twentieth-Century American Poetry*, editors Jack Myers and David Wojahn present a collection of essays that trace the development of American poetry from 1908 to the 1990s. What clearly emerges from reading this study is that White writers before the 1960s did not look to Black poets when they sought craftsmen or to women poets as role models and that the major influences on twentieth-century White American poetry are Walt Whitman, Emily Dickinson, Robert Frost, T. S. Eliot, and Wallace Stevens. If we are going to be successful at identifying a theory of African-American poetry, we must look to the works of our own writers and develop the theory from within our tradition, from their works and not from the outside. We must not follow the established trend of Black theoreticians who have theorized about fiction by imposing alien terminology from outside the culture, or who have cleverly taken an African folktale and imbued it with Eurocentric intellectual thought that has nothing to do with the culture from which the tale is taken.

The nature of our poetic tradition demands that criticism and theory of Black poetry be grounded in Black folk or popular culture. Because of the elitist nature of Eurocentric critical theory, Black writers who have suggested that our folk culture is the source of our literature have been perceived as either propagandistic or negligent in   addressing aesthetic issues. The critical ideas of

Langston Hughes, Richard Wright, Larry Neal, Hoyt Fuller, Addison Gayle, and Stephen Henderson, from varying perspectives, have demonstrated that folk speech (rural, urban, folktales), music (spirituals, folk songs, blues, jazz), religion (sermons, Islam, Christianity), and liberation politics (freedom from oppression in the diaspora and in Africa) are the elements of an African-American poetic aesthetics.

The most engaging and widely known study to address the aesthetics of African-American poetry is Kimberly Benston's "Performing Blackness: Re/Placing Afro-American Poetry," collected in *Afro-American Literary Study in the 1990s* (1989). Although this essay demonstrates the serious thought that African-American poetry demands, it also reflects the dangers of a contemporary theoretical process and language that operate at a high level of abstraction and fail to move beyond the level of theorizing. Benston writes,"...a division persists between our knowledge of the poetry as text and our awareness of it as performance" (165). Ironically, perhaps the most important characteristic of our poetry is its orality, the transformation of words into performance. However, my use of performance here is not synonymous with Benston's use of the term. In contemporary theoretical parlance, *performance*, the noun form of *performative* refers to "a kind of utterance that performs with language the deed to which it refers . . . instead of describing some state of affairs" (164). Thus Benston calls for a metalinguistic analysis of Black poetry that never moves beyond discussions of language about language.

Such discussions of the performative act of Black poetry must move beyond exclusively intellectual exercises about the intricacies of language to analyses that merge aesthetics with political commitment and meaning. Benston's essay rejects the entire social, political, and cultural content that underlie the conception of most Black poetry. He explains:

> I think we need to see Afro-American poetry not
> as a static alignment of proclamations (reflecting
> either some preconstituted "reality" *or* its own
> stagnant pool of tropes) but rather as a perfor-
> mative activity that sees itself in struggle with
> other practices. A corollary point: we must rec-
> ognize our own relation to this process, under-
> standing interpretation as an inescapably medi-
> atory act that will itself be a transformative
> process. Thus, as we contemplate our move-
> ment past the juncture of Black Arts and formal-
> ist impulses that situates much of our work
> today, we must be careful not to retreat into a
> nostalgic humanism which ignores the differ-
> ences *within* black discourse(s) as well as their
> conflicts with other discourses. Conventional
> oppositions of praxis/theory and history/dis-
> course which occupy so much of our internecine
> exchanges will no longer serve. Our readings *are*
> performances which theorize their relations to
> other readings. They, too, continuously (re) con-
> struct their "subjects." (182-83)

Numerous questions beg for answers here. What is
the purpose of theorizing about the relationship of our performances to other readings? What is the purpose of discourse? If interpretation is "an inescapably mediatory act
that will itself be a transformative process," what is this
process being transformed into? In other words, why are
we critics engaged in the critical process? If our words are
limited to the academy, why is it that we do not use them
as a process or means by which we can change the academy so that it becomes more involved in what's happening
in the outside world of which the academy is a part? Only
those of us from a privileged group or who identify with
such a group would call humanism "nostalgic." Real

humanism has yet to be realized on this planet, in this country.

Why is it that instead of refining, retuning, or reshaping what is defined as those weaknesses of the Black Aesthetic, we immerse ourselves deeper in the very Eurocentric aesthetic the theoreticians of the Black Arts Movement fought against? Haki Madhubuti's comments succinctly capture the essence of the Black aesthetic creed. He says, "Writers write. What they write about tells the reader to what extent they are involved with the real world....Writers should be questioners of the world and doers within the world" (*Capsule* 21). Most of our creative artists, and particularly our poets, have stressed in their works the need for Black creative artists to maintain connections to their people, not to "metapeople." J. Saunders Redding's presentation of the essential qualities of good poetry analogously describes the qualities necessary for the critic or theorist of Black poetry if the scholar intends to remain inside the tradition of African-American poetry. Saunders says, "The essential quality of good poetry is utmost sincerity and earnestness of purpose. A poet untouched by his times, by his conditions, by his environment is only half poet, for earnestness and sincerity grow in direct proportion as one feels intelligently the pressure of immediate life" (108-09).

The most immediate cultural environment for the scholar of African-American poetry is the poetry itself with its political and linguistic or verbal consistencies that have endured for well over a century. The terminology we use to theorize or critique African-American literature, in this case poetry, should come from within Africa or Black culture in the diaspora. A method I propose is one that uses terms taken from the Charleston, South Carolina, area where an incredibly large number of African slaves were taken whose homes were in Angola, Gambia, the Congo, Sierra Leone, Senegambia, and Guinea. At lease 70 percent of all incoming Africans into South Carolina were Bantu from the Angola region near the Congo River. "For [these] Africans in South Carolina, the first stage in the acculturation process was the melting of numerous West and Central African elements in a culture such as Gullah. The creation of this Creole culture allowed these Africans to form a kind of lingua franca, enabling them to communicate with each other as well as with the planters" (Holloway 9). Consequently, the largest and most homogeneous group in the area, the Bantu had great influence over other African groups in the area. "Also, since the Bantus were predominantly field hands or were used in capacities that required little or no contact with European-Americans, they were not confronted with the problem of acculturation, as the West African domestic servants and artisans were. Coexisting in relative isolation from other groups, the Bantus were able to maintain a strong sense of unity and to retain a cultural vitality that laid the foundation for the development of African-American culture" (Holloway 9).

Continuing the Bantus' tradition of unity and affirming their strong cultural identity, in the title of this essay and in the exploration to follow, I use the word *bantu* to refer to those characteristics of Black speech such as plantation, rural and urban dialect, folktales, sermons, the dozens, signifying, and all other historical characteristics of Black speech, such as those listed by Stephen Henderson in his *Understanding the New Black Poetry*.

The Bantus were clearly a political people. This political consciousness and a deeply spiritual component have always been integral aspects of African-American poetry. The most pervading aspect of late nineteenth and early twentieth-century African-American poetry that manifest to date is the theme of liberation or consciousness raising against the evils of oppression. I refer to this characteristic as *Nkodi*, a Bakongo word for specialists who sent messages to the dead (Holloway 152). The *nkodi* are closely related to the *Nganga*, in Bakongo a priest who employed life-affirming nkisi to heal and ward off *kindoki* (evil). Thus in the Bantu cultures in the diaspora as well as in Africa, the religious and the political are intertwined. In the tradition of African-American poetry, politics and Christianity are sometimes wedded together as they are in the poetry of Francis Harper, James Whitfield, and Margaret Walker, or they are diametrically at odds as they are in some of the poetry of Frank Marshall Davis, Amiri Baraka, and Haki Madhubuti. Henry Dumas' contribution infuses an understanding of African spirituality with consciousness raising.

Instead of following the tradition of isolation and despair that characterizes much contemporary Euro-American poetry, African-American poetry celebrates life, is life-affirming. African music on the continent and in the diaspora also reflects this affirmation of life. And although James Edwin Campbell and Paul Laurence Dunbar perfected the use of dialect before Langston Hughes, Hughes was the first to bring the blues and jazz rhythms to Black poetry in America. Following Hughes and Sterling Brown, many of the poets of the 1960s who are still writing and reciting today—Nikki Giovanni, Haki Madhubuti, Eugene Redmond, Amiri Baraka, and Sonia Sanchez—perform their poetry with musical groups. Music not only becomes part of the subject matter of their poetry, it also appears in the typography of the poem and in the poets' use of their voices or, in what some would refer to as, their utterances. This use of music as a group activity continues the African tradition. In discussing the function of music in African societies, Kwabena Nketia writes, "...music making is generally organized as a social event. Public performances, therefore, take place on social occasions—that is, on occasions when members of a group or a community come together for the enjoyment of leisure, for recreational activities, or for the performance of a rite, ceremony, festival, or any kind of collective activity" (Nketia 21).

As in Africa, music is integral to all aspects of African-American life as demonstrated by the development of our musical tradition, which includes folk spirituals, folk gospels, gospel choirs, gospel quartets, contemporary gospel, work songs, field songs, protest songs, game songs, social songs, rural blues, ragtime, vaudeville blues, boogie-woogie, New Orleans jazz, big bands, rhythm and blues, urban blues, bebop, rock 'n' roll, soul, soul jazz, civil rights songs, jazz fusion, funk, disco, rap, techno funk, go-go, and house music. I use the word *ndungu*, the name of the long drums used in Haitian dance with their origins in the Kongo or Zaire.

In this essay, I would like to explore the predominance and merger of *bantu* (Black speech), *nganga* (Religion), *ndungu* (music), and *nkodi* (politics) in African-American poetry by providing a brief overview of the prevailing subjects and stylistic features of the poetry in four seminal and available anthologies of African-American literature: *Black Writers of America, The New Cavalcade: African-American Writing from 1760 to the Present*, and *In the Tradition: An Anthology of Young Black Writers*. I offer here a practical interpretive piece, based on a specific theory of interpretation. Such an approach takes African-American literary theory out of the realm of abstraction, where words and utterances only refer to a more involved level of words and utterances, and secures the interpretive act inside the tradition of African-American literary history. When Stephen Henderson says in his response to Benson's essay that the challenge of the modern world requires sophisticated African-American criticism (192) of Black poetry, he had already made it clear that this criticism, in order to be a part of the continuing tradition, must maintain its cultural, folk, and popular roots (192). So the dilemma which emerges is how do we keep our folk base, which demands a kind of humanism that has been under attack for years in the Eurocentric academy, and at the same time focus on aesthetics with the "sophistication" that moves us beyond the 1960s.

Addressing the politics of academia and those of the world discussed in the writer's art is an essential aspect of the paradigm I propose here. It is the absence of this polit-ical component that enables contemporary theoreticians to ignore the environmental background of Black fiction and poetry. This political component demands that we talk/write about how we treat each other (our humanism or our lack of it) and that we address the inherent hypocrisy of a literary endeavor that seeks to be solely metaphysical. As for formalism, any reader who peruses my book on Richard Wright's *Native Son* and sees nothing that goes beyond Aristotle's *Poetics* or grammatical, gener-ic, and syntactical form also refuses to examine the merger of politics and aesthetics, a process which privileges nei-ther form nor content.

Although post-structuralist theories are to be celebrat-ed for disrupting assumptions and predictable reading pat-terns in fiction, they do not provide the direction we need to address the merger of Black speech, politics, religion, and music in our art, especially our poetry. For all of these characteristics of Black poetry have at their roots Black sur-vival. They emerged and continue to thrive in a context that is always environmentally and socially grounded.

The four previously listed anthologies demonstrate the folk origins of African-American poetry which emerge as a people's expressive responses to the social, political, psychological forces that dominate their lives. The folk songs (both secular and sacred), of course, precede Phillis Wheatley and her learned poetry. Thus while much of con-temporary African-American poetry, especially the poetry by the young writers collected in Kevin Powell and Ras Baraka's *In the Tradition*, reflects the stylistic features of an African oral tradition, which manifests in folk songs and early folk poetry, African-American poetry has also devel-oped intermittently through the works of those poets who, like Wheatley, perfected the Eurocentric features of their poetry. James Monroe Whitfield, Frances Harper, Paul Laurence Dunbar, William Stanley Braithwaite, Fenton Johnson, Georgia Douglas Johnson, Countee Cullen, Claude McKay, Melvin Tolson, Owen Dodson, Samuel Allen, Robert Hayden, and Gwendolyn Brooks are examples of some of these poets who, before the influences of the Black Arts Movement of the 1960s, crafted their art primarily on the models of mainstream poetry. Contemporary Black poetry reflects the merger of the tenets of the Black Aesthetic and Eurocentric features. This wedding is characterized by some combination of the presence of Black speech, music, religion, and politics, the characteristics of folk poetry.

Dudley Randall begins his edition of *Black Poets* with folk poetry, which he divides into folk seculars and spirituals. Even a cursory glance at the titles and content of these secular folk songs reveals the slaves' outrage over the conditions that stifle their lives. Songs such as "He Paid Me Seven," "Run, Nigger, Run," "Promises of Freedom," "Song to the Runaway Slave," and "The Old Section Boss" combine folk speech, music, and political commitment, while folk spirituals such as "Go Down, Moses," "Josha Fit De Battle of Jericho," "Steal Away to Jesus," and many others illuminate how Biblical stories and allusions serve as parables to the slaves' reaction to their bondage.

While *The New Cavalcade* does not include a separate section on folk poetry, Keneth Kinnaman and Richard Barksdale's well-known *Black Writers of America* has four sections of folk poetry that records folk poetry from the seventeenth century to the 1970s. Thus *Black Poets* and *Black Writers of America* demonstrate the folk origins and continuum of the folk tradition in African-American poetry. More contemporary and comprehensive than Randall's and the Barksdale-Kinnamon anthologies, *The New Cavalcade* provides an overview of the historical development of African-American literature, including sixty-two poets that span the centuries from Phillis Wheatley to E. Ethelbert Miller. Before Langston Hughes' poetry, no one poem reflects the merger of music, politics, religion, and Black speech, although many poems reflect the presence of any one of these features.

The idea that Phillis Wheatley does not concern herself with the issue of slavery is now in literary circles an unlearned cliche that was dispelled by critics like John C. Shields. In fact, some of Phillis Wheatley's poetry is equally political as that of James Monroe Whitfield and George Moses Horton. Her poem "To the University of Cambridge, in New England" confirms the subtlety that describes her political voice. Addressed to the students at the university, the poem warns them that morality, virtue, and religion must not be shunned for knowledge and education. The poem's last stanza captures Wheatley's subtle, almost camouflaged critique of White society:

> Ye blooming plants of human race divine,
> An *Ethiop* tells you 'tis your greatest foe;
> Its transient sweetness turns to endless pain,
> And in immense perdition sinks the soul. (12)

It is highly ironic that one brought to America to be a slave and thus perceived by the students as inferior is the one to tell the students that the joys of sin, their greatest foe, are transient. The lines "Remember, Christians, Negroes, black as Cain/May be refin'd, and join th' angelic train" found at the end of "On Being Brought from Africa to America" confirms Wheatley's condemnation of racial oppression. Because of the presence of religious faith and her use of it to challenge mainstream notions of virtue and morality, Phillis Wheatley, then, is both at the beginning and the center of the African-American poetic tradition.

Following Wheatley, James Whitfield and Frances

Harper wrote more overt political poetry. But a name less
known than theirs is James Edwin Campbell, a master of
the plantation dialect before Paul Laurence Dunbar. The
few poems of Campbell collected in *The New Cavalcade*
illustrate his sharp ear for plantation dialect and the connection between music and religion in the plantation's cultural life. Quite similar to Campbell's poetry, Paul
Laurence Dunbar's frequently anthologized "An Ante-
Bellum Sermon" illustrates, like the spirituals, how the
slaves used religion to camouflage their condemnation of
slavery. Using Moses' successful defeat of Pharaoh as the
crux of his sermon, the preacher denies that his words have
any meaning outside the Biblical story:

> An' de lan' shall hyeah his thunder,
>   lak a blas' fom Gab'el's ho'n,
> Fu' de Lawd of hosts is mighty
>   When he girds his ahmor on.
> But fu' feah some one mistakes me,
>   I will pause right hyeah to say,
> Dat I'm still a'preachin' ancient,
>   I ain't talkin' 'bout to-day. (303)

The preacher clearly knows that he must protect himself an
that he cannot trust everyone indiscriminately in his audience. Although he is not educated in the fashion of Phillis
Wheatley, he uses a rhetorical technique similar to paralip-
sis. Telling his audience something that he says he is not
going to tell them, he ironically denies that his sermon
relates at all to the slave masters.

In addition to "An Ante-Bellum Sermon," the most
anthologized of Dunbar's poetry are the poems "When
Malindy Sings," "Sympathy," and "We Wear the Mask."
Like his "Ode to Ethiopia," collected in *The New Cavalcade*
both "Sympathy" and "We Wear the Mask" address the
African-Americans' reaction to their oppression. Recorded
in African-American literary history as some of the most

well-honed poetry, Paul Laurence Dunbar's poetry manifests the features of religion, music, language, and political
commitment. Just as Dunbar is the first African-American
poet to make a living from his writing, he is also the first to
integrate these features throughout his canon. His ear for
the plantation dialect in "An Ante-Bellum Sermon," "When
Malindy Sings," and many other dialect poems brings a
melody and rhythm to African-American poetry   that
remained unchallenged until Langston Hughes' blues and
jazz poetry.

In his masterful adaptation of urban Black folk speech
and his transformation of blues and jazz music into a literary form, Langston Hughes emerges as the artist whose
works are a culmination of the folk songs and folk poetry
and of Paul Laurence Dunbar's plantation dialect pieces.
Consequently, in tracing the continuum in African-
American poetry, Langston Hughes had the same irrevocable influence in the twentieth century that Dunbar had on
Black poetry in the late nineteenth century. Although it is
undeniable that numerous other poets of the Harlem
Renaissance, such as Claude McKay, Countee Cullen,
Georgia Douglas Johnson, Alice Dunbar-Nelson, Anne
Spencer, Helene Johnson, Gwendolyn Bennett, Effie Lee
Newson, and others were skillful poets, Langston Hughes
emerged as a poet "of the people," and, for numerous rea-
sons, we now distinguish him from the group.

In the 1920s, publishers were clearly interested in
Black male writers who highlighted racial issues in their
art. Both McKay and Cullen wrote poems, such as McKay's
"Spring in New Hampshire" and Cullen's "To John Keats,
Poet, At Springtime" that have nothing to do with racial
issues, but they are best remembered for those poems that
do. Mckay's sonnets such as "Harlem Shadows" and "If We
Must Die" and Cullen's "Heritage" and "Yet Do I Marvel"
are their most anthologized pieces. Women writers of the
Harlem Renaissance, like Georgia Douglas Johnson, Anne

Spencer, and others are far less visible than McKay and
Cullen in the annuals of literary history because their most
frequently anthologized poems address such subjects as
love, death, pain, and the futility of war. Maureen Honey's
edition of *Shadowed Dreams: Women's Poetry of the Harlem
Renaissance* remains the only anthology that provides a
broad coverage of the women poets of the Renaissance.
Part II of the anthology subtitled "Heritage" presents twenty-five poems that have Black life as their subject. These
poems focus on the beauty of Black life and thus lack the
rebelliousness or anger that describes McKay's and
Cullen's poems. Because most anthologies of Harlem
Renaissance writers either ignore the women poets or publish those poems that do not emphasize blackness, most
readers think that these women neglected to write on racial
subjects.

The politics of the times, literary history, and his
unsurpassed genius have made Langston Hughes one of
the most widely known poets of his time and ours. Despite
an understandably small Black reading audience, Hughes'
poems were addressed to Blacks as well as Whites.
However, the voice he uses in most of his poems—those
written in dialect and those written in standard usage—is
the voice of the common person. His "Theme for English
B" and the companion pieces "Low to High" and "High to
Low" demonstrate how Hughes could take standard
English and transform it into a form that lies between Black
dialect proper and standard English. The first two lines of
"Negro Dancers," "Me an' ma baby's/Got two mo' ways,"
compared to the lines "How can you low-rate me /this
way?" from "Low to High" illustrate my point here.

As is the case with much of Hughes' poetry, "Theme
for English B," "Low to High," and "High to Low" address
the ramifications of racism. While the two companion
pieces highlight the intraracial class conflict within the
Black community, "Theme for English B" informs White

society that the Black man and woman are as much American as the White man or woman: "You are white—/yet a part of me, as I am a part of you." Hughes captures the African-American's historical journey to America in what is perhaps his signature poem "The Negro Speaks of Rivers." Dedicated to W E.B. DuBois and using water or the river as a metaphor for the source of life (Black life), the poem traces the movement of Black life from the Euphrates and Nile rivers in Africa to the Mississippi river. Hughes subtlety couches his admonishment of slavery and racism in the refrain "My soul has grown deep like the rivers." The first time the line appears in the poem it follows the poet's assertion that he has known rivers "ancient as the world and older than the flow of/human blood in human veins." The poet here identifies himself and his blackness with the first human beings. The second and only other time the line appears in the poem occurs after the poet has made reference to Mississippi, New Orleans, and Abe Lincoln. He places the lines "My soul has grown deep like the rivers" at the end of the poem, this time suggesting that he is no longer the same man who "bathed in the Euphrates" and "built [his] hut near the Congo." He is now a Black man who has experienced the pain of slavery and racism, and his soul now bears the imprint of these experiences.

So far the poems discussed above reveal Langston Hughes's political commitment and make some suggestions about his use of Black speech. But one of the poems that best captures the full range of the stylistic innovations Hughes brings to African-American poetry and identifies him as the prototype for the Black Arts Movement of the late 1960s is "The Cat and the Saxophone." Because the poem is short and all its elements inextricably interwoven, I cite it in full:

EVERYBODY
Half-pint,—
Gin?
No, make it
LOVES MY BABY
corn. You like
liquor,
don't you honey?
BUT MY BABY
Sure. Kiss me,
DON'T LOVE NOBODY
daddy.
BUT ME.
Say!
EVERYBODY
Yes?
WANTS MY BABY
I'm your
BUT MY BABY
sweetie, ain't I?
DON'T WANT NOBODY
Sure.
BUT
Then let's
ME,
do it!
SWEET ME.
Charleston,
mamma!
!

The scene of the poem is a jazz club at two o'clock in the morning, and, of course, the cat is the man talking to his woman or someone he wants to be his woman. As the man raps to the woman, a saxophone player performs. And either he or someone else sings the blues lyrics that Hughes represents in capital letters. The poem is a tightly integrated network that vacillates between the dialogue between the man and the woman and the words of the singer. In addition to being the lyrics to the blues songs, the words in all capitals also set the rhythm of the poem as they capture the saxophone's melody.

"The Cat and the Saxophone" exemplifies all those qualities of Hughes' poems that presage the Black poetry of the 1960s. Although Sterling Brown, too, perfected transforming blues music into poetic form and captured with a sharp ear the urban and rural Black speech, it was Langston Hughes who opened up its possibilities for Black poetry with much the same effect Richard Wright achieved in fiction. The features of music (blues, jazz), language (Black speech), religion, and political commitment summarize the predominant stylistic and thematic characteristics of Hughes' poetry. Despite the fact that *The New Cavalcade* does not include any of Hughes' poems, such as "Prayer Meeting," "Feet o' Jesus," "Angels Wings," "Judgment Day," and "Prayer," the reader familiar with African-American culture knows that the mother in the frequently anthologized poem "Mother to Son" is steeped in a religious faith that is her ideological foundation and gives her the power to tell her son not to expect life to be a crystal stair.

The daughter of a Methodist minister and educated in church schools, Margaret Walker joins Sterling Brown, Robert Hayden, and Gwendolyn Brooks as four well-known Black poets, whose initial publications followed Langston Hughes and preceded the Black Arts Movement. Like Phillis Wheatley, the stylistic features of Gwendolyn Brooks' and Robert Hayden's poems reveal their success at honing Eurocentric poetic forms. And also like Wheatley, their subject matter manifests a political commitment that comprises part of the continuum of the African-American poetic tradition. Moreover, Brooks shares a passion for ballads with Sterling Brown and Margaret Walker. Such ballads as Brooks' "Ballad of Pearl Mae Lee," "Brown's "Old Lem," and Walker's "Ballad for Phillis Wheatley" confirm their use of music and/or Black speech as poetic references.

The content of these poems positions them at the center of a poetic tradition that attacks racial oppression. Brooks' "Ballad of Pearl Mae Lee" in its focus on the White woman's betrayal of the Black man and Brown's "Old Lem" in its concentration on the overwhelming force the White world wields over Black society address contemporary racial issues.

Although they both began publishing their work in the 1940s, Gwendolyn Brooks and Margaret Walker continue to write and publish poetry that reflects the influences of the times and experiences through which they have lived. In her *Report from Part I*, Brooks documents her first encounter with Amiri Baraka and the ideology of the Black Arts Movement. Manifesting the influence of the new movement, Brooks, after 1967, no longer used the sonnet form, which is so pervasive in her early poetry.

Students of African-American literature sometimes fail to realize that more mature poets, like Gwendolyn Brooks, Margaret Walker, Lance Jeffers, Dudley Randall, and Robert Hayden, also make up the Black poetic tradition of the 1960s. In fact, a look at the single, most important publication of the Black Arts Movement in the 1960s, Amiri Baraka and Larry Neal's edition of *Black Fire: An Anthology of Afro-American Writing*, reveals that a number of the poets in this volume did not survive the test of time. Despite the fact that Gwendolyn Brooks, Margaret Walker, Lance Jeffers, Dudley Randall, and Robert Hayden were never identified with the Black Arts Movement as defined by Baraka and Neal, these older poets have all made their indelible mark on the African-American poetic tradition.

While some younger, contemporary writers, such as Trey Ellis, attempt to replace the Black Aesthetic or Black Arts Movement with what Ellis refers to as the *New Black Aesthetic*, the Black Aesthetic Movement of the 1960s and early 1970s changed the course of African-American poetry irrevocably. Following the lead of Black jazz musicians

Ornette Coleman, Sonny Rollins, Pharaoh Sanders, Sun Ra, and John Coltrane, Black poets with Amiri Baraka, Larry Neal, Sarah Webster Fabio, Sonia Sanchez, Haki Madhubuti, and Nikki Giovanni in the vanguard began to redefine themselves and their poetry by grounding their art in Black speech and Black music. Taking up the legacy handed to them by Langston Hughes, these young poets were far more outspoken than he about their intent to merge the political and the aesthetic in shaping their art. They went further than Hughes in making it clear that they were addressing a Black audience with the goal of spiritual awakening and sharpening political consciousness.

The four landmark publications that present the political and aesthetic ideology of the Black Aesthetic are the already mentioned *Black Fire* (1968); Addison Gayle's edition of *The Black Aesthetic* (1971); Stephen Henderson's *Understanding the New Black Poetry* (1972); and a series of essays published in the *Negro Digest* from September 1968 to November 1969. Except for Henderson's collection, the anthologies include literary critics, dramatists, and fiction writers. Yet, it was the poets who were at the vanguard of this movement. Haki Madhubuti, Keorapetse Kgositsile, Carolyn Rodgers, and Sarah Webster Fabio, all have essays in these late 1960s issues of *Negro Digest* where they discuss the technique and direction of Black poetry. These essays discuss stylistic innovations and particularly Black subjects that challenge Euro-American definitions and expectations of poetry.

Although these young poets redefined Black poetry in the 1960s, the essential component of their art manifests the same integration of music, language, religion, and politics that constitutes the development of Black poetry from Phillis Wheatley to the present day. Their contributions emerge as a sharpened political focus and an innovative honing of their use of Black speech and Black music.

A look at Haki Madhubuti's poem "blackmusic/a

beginning," taken from his 1969 collection Don't Cry,
Scream reveals the deepened integration of aesthetics and
political commitment:

    pharaoh sanders
    had
    finished
    playing
    &
    the whi-
    te boy was to
    go on next.

    him didn't
    him sd
    that
    his horn
    was
    broke.

    they sat
    there
    dressed in
    african garb
    & dark sun glasses
    listening to the brothers
    play.   (taking notes)
    we
    didn't realize
    who they
    were un
    til their
    next recording
    had been
    released: the beach boys play soulmusic.

    real sorry about
    the supremes
    being dead,

> heard some whi
> te girls
> the other day—
> all wigged—down
> with a mean tan—
> soundin just like them,
> singin
> rodgers & hart
> & some country & western. (*Don't Cry,*
>   *Scream* 48-49)

Published before Little Richard began to talk incessantly about how his music was taken from him by Whites, before television began to use James Brown's and the Temptations music for its commercials, before many of the older blues musicians spoke publicly on talk shows about their exploitation, this poem signifies on White society's attempt to usurp an art form that is inherently alien to European culture. Any discussion of this poem that ignores Black exploitation and the thoughts, feelings, and cultural rebellion, which provide the roots for jazz, is one that refuses to move beyond the metaphysical, the martial arts of discussing language about language.   Of course, the typography of the poem, the poet's refusal to use capital letters, his blending of words together as in "soulmusic," demonstrate how Madhubuti moves beyond Langston Hughes' and Sterling Brown's adaptation of rural and urban Black dialects. Whereas Hughes' and Brown's spellings reflect their effort to capture the sounds of Black speech, Madhubuti and most of his contemporaries not only captured Black speech, they also defied Euro-American academic standards by deliberately adopting unstandardized, anti-middle class poetic forms.

This defiance of Euro-American aesthetic standards reflects the 1960s poets political commitment to move away from the White mainstream's cultural expectations. Thus the traditional focus on religion that imbued Phillis

Wheatley's, Dunbar's, Hughes, and Margaret Walker's poetry was replaced by a rejection of Christianity and the adoption of Islam. Many of these writers, such as Sonia Sanchez, who in the early 1970s was associated with the Nation of Islam and later moved away from the group, manifested an interest in spirituality that went beyond institutionalized religion.

The focus on spirituality centered on African history with particular attention given to traditional African religions. An essential component of this return to African culture emerges in the manner in which poets, like Sanchez, Baraka, Giovanni, and others read their poetry. Their dramatic performance finds its source, like the folk songs and folk poetry, in the oral tradition in African culture. Almost all of these poets identified with the 1960s Black Arts Movement and those who joined their company in the 1970s, 1980s, and 1990s demonstrate the indigenous African oral tradition in Black poetry through various combinations of references to African history and Egyptian gods and goddesses, the accompaniment of spirituals, jazz, blues, African percussions, and chanting.

Perhaps nothing better demonstrates how the 1960s and 1970s poets enriched the legacy they received from Langston Hughes and Sterling Brown than the contrast between Sanchez' reading/performance of her poetry and Langston Hughes' reading of his. Fortunately, literary archives provide us with a few recordings of Langston Hughes' readings of his poetry. They are rather dry and casual with very little attempt at dramatic effect. Influenced by Hughes's transformation of blues and jazz into literary art, the Black poets of the 1960s enriched this poetic legacy by extending the transformation so that the performance of the poem itself becomes a jazz or blues song or an African chant. Although Haki Madhubuti, Amiri Baraka, Eugene Redmond, Jayne Cortez, Quincy Troupe, and Nikki Giovanni all deliver spellbinding readings of their poetry, Sonia Sanchez emerges as the priestess whose performances combine music, religion, politics, and Black speech so ingeniously that she brings to these historical characteristics a heightened aesthetics. In her performance of any number of her poems—"Kwa mama zetu waliotuza," "Letter to Dr. Martin Luther King"—she challenges the listeners'/readers' Eurocentric perception of reality by calling on the spirits of the ancestors to heal Black people's physical and psychological wounds and to enlighten their political awareness. These incantations forbid indifference or political neutrality from Whites as well as Blacks, but their Black speech, their psychological emphases, and their origins in African culture suggest that a Black audience is Sanchez' primary focus.

Even the titles of the works of the poets in the vanguard of the Black Arts Movement illustrate the writers' goal of awakening the spiritual and political consciousness of a Black audience. Amiri Baraka's *Black Art, Black Magic, It's Nation Time*, Mari Evans' *Where Is All the Music?*, Carolyn Rodgers' *Song of the Blackbird*, Sonia Sanchez' *Home Coming, We a BaddDDD People, Blues Book for Blue Black Magical Women*, and Haki Madhubuti's *Think Black, Black Pride*, and *Don't Cry, Scream* reflect the momentum to which these poets used their art to expose the social, political, and psychological impediments to Black well-being. To affirm their connection with their African heritage, some of these writers and those that followed changed their Euro-American names to African or Arabic names: For example, Don L. Lee became Haki R. Madhubuti, Rolland Snellings became Askia Toure, Jewell Latimore became Johari Amini, Paulette Williams became Ntozake Shange, and LeRoi Jones became Amiri Baraka.

Perhaps, no poet better demonstrates the presence of Black music, Black speech, politics, and religion in contemporary African-American poetry than Amiri Baraka's son Ras Baraka. Because most of the poets who came into the limelight in the 1960s continue to dominate the African-American poetic arena, Ras Baraka, twenty-four years old and already an accomplished poet, and his generation both confirm the irrevocable influence and contributions of his father's generation to African-American poetry and presage the direction of that poetry. The 1990s has so far produced four anthologies of African-American poetry: Michael Harper and Anthony Walton's *Every Shut Eye Ain't Sleep: An Anthology of Poetry by African-Americans Since 1945*, E. Ethelbert Miller's *In Search of Color Everywhere: A Collection of African-American Poetry*, Clarence Major's *The Garden Thrives: Twentieth-Century African-American Poetry*, and Kevin Powell and Ras Baraka's *In the Tradition: An Anthology of Young Black Writers*.

The title of Powell and Ras Baraka's anthology clearly distinguishes it from the others, which present the works of older, better known poets. At even a slight glance, the typography of the poems in *In the Tradition* substantiates the virtuosic (to use one of Stephen Henderson's terms) free verse that best describes the arrangement of Black poetry in the 1990s. Ras Baraka's poem "In The Tradition Too," dedicated to Amiri and Amina Baraka, powerfully recalls a tradition in African-American poetry in which politics and aesthetics are inextricably interwoven.

Using the title of one of his father's well-known poems "In the Tradition," Ras Baraka's "In The Tradition Too" (which is much like Amiri Baraka's poem "Black Art") is a poetic manifesto that uses Black political and literary history as sources for Black strength and survival. This "African war song" includes references to various types of African-American music, such as spirituals, blues, and jazz; references to rap artists, such as Flavor Flav and Public Enemy, Big Daddy Kane, and Melody; and to rap recordings, like "Rebel Without a Pause" and "Stop the Violence"; and references to reggae musicians, such as Bob Marley and Steele Pulse. While the spirituals and blues are creative outcomes

of the pain of racial oppression, jazz, reggae, and rap
evolve as rhythmical and vocal attacks on racial oppression, imperialism, capitalism, and the like. Ras Baraka
places these musicians in a "tradition of workers and fighters" whose resistance joins forces with literary fighters,
such as his father, W. E. B. Du Bois, Toni Cade Bambara,
Toni Morrison, Sonia Sanchez, Langston Hughes, James
Baldwin, and his own mother, Amini.

Echoing Haki Madhubuti's collection of poetry entitled *Killing Memory, Seeking Ancestors* and serving the same
purpose as Sanchez' chants, this poem announces that the
poet pays the debt of memory to all those who were
enslaved and lynched. Typical of Black poetry of the sixties, "In The Tradition Too" catalogs those situations and
Black figures whose lives have made an impact in the
struggle against racism both nationally and international-
ly. He includes Tawana Brawley and Howard Beach,
Malcolm X, Medgar Evers, Martin Luther King Jr., Patrice
Lumumba, Fred Hampton, George Jackson, and Kwame
Nkrumah. This catalog of national and international figures reflects the poet's communal, global, or Pan-African
aim of bringing the worldwide Black family together under
one umbrella of identification and resistance.

The poem ends on a note of resistance and the commitment to building heritage:

> I wanna be blackness, I wanna be peace.
> I wanna be Amiri and Amini too. I wanna
> be both of you! And I will carry the
> tradition on in good times and bad and build
> and create, create and build, build and create
> and create and build.........
> THE KLAN WILL DIE AND
> BLACK PEOPLE WILL BE VICTORIOUS! (89)

Reminiscent of both the Black power and Black is
beautiful slogans of the 1960s, these last lines demonstrate

the message of the entire poem. The son of two of the most well-known figures in African-American poetic history, Ras Baraka pays tribute to his mother and father—his literary ancestors—who bequeathed him a tradition in which poet and political activist are one. Ras Baraka's use of anadiplosis (the repetition of the last word of one clause at the beginning of the following clause) and polysyndeton (use of many conjunctions) extends the length of lines so that form and meaning are parallel. He and the lines build heritage.

This Pan-African heritage focuses inward exclusively on Black people. The Klan becomes a symbol of all those forces that conspire to ignore, distort, or destroy the multi-faceted Black tradition. If Black people worldwide are to be victorious as the poet suggests at the end, then all areas of African-American intellectual, political, social, and psychological lives must be directed toward Black survival. A major source of strength and inspiration, the continuum in African-American poetry, from Phillis Wheatley to Ras Baraka, reflects the interrelationship of Black speech, music, religion, and politics as poetic references. In keeping with this tradition, any theory of African-American poetry must be an outgrowth of a careful study of those expressive attributes that recur most frequently. Using the words in the title of this essay, I refer to attributes found in the Charleston, South Carolina area because the cultural or expressive lives of the slaves who populated this region reflected a determination to "rebuild" their African heritage and a political understanding of the need for group identity. In continuing this tradition of looking inward, bantu (language), nkodi (politics), ndungu (music), and nganga (religion) offer a linguistic paradigm for keeping African-American poetry "In The Tradition Too."

WORKS CITED

Baraka, Ras. "In the Tradition Too." In *In the Tradition: An Anthology of Young Black Writers*. Ed. Kevin Powell and Ras Baraka. New York: Writers & Readers Publishing, Inc., 1992.

Benston, Kimberly. "Performing Blackness: Re/Placing Afro-American Poetry." In *Afro-American Literary Study in the 1990s*. Ed. Houston A. Baker, Jr. and Patricia Redmond. Chicago: U of Chicago P, 1989.

Dunbar, Paul Laurence. "An Ante-Bellum Sermon." In *The New Cavalcade: African-American Writing from 1760 to the Present*. Ed. Arthur P. Davis, Saunders Redding, and Joyce A. Joyce. Vol. 1. Washington, DC: Howard U P, 1991. 2 vols. 1991-92.

Holloway, Joseph. "The Origins of African-American Culture." In *Africanisms in American Culture*. Ed. Joseph Holloway. Bloomington: Indiana U P, 1990. 1-19.

Hughes, Langston. "The Cat and the Saxophone ; High to Low ; Low to High ; The Negro Speaks of Rivers. In *The New Cavalcade: African-American Writing from 1960 to the Present*. Ed. Arthur P. Davis, Saunders Redding, and Joyce A. Joyce. Vol. 1. Washington, DC: Howard U P, 1991. 2 vols. 1991-92.

Madhubuti, Haki. "Haki Madhubuti (Don L. Lee)." In *A Capsule Course in Black Poetry Writing*. Detroit: Broadside Press, 1975. 21-34.

_____. "blackmusic/a beginning." In *Don't Cry, Scream*.

Chicago: Third World Press, 1969. Rpt. Chicago: Third World Press, 1992.

Nketia, Kwabena. *The Music of Africa*. New York: Norton, 1974. 21-50.

Redding, Saunders. *To Make a Poet Black*. Chapel, N.C.: U of North Carolina P, 1939. Rpt. Ithaca, NY: 1988.

Wheatley, Phillis. "To the University of Cambridge, In New England." In *The New Cavalcade: African-American Writing from 1760 to the Present*. Ed. Arthur P. Davis, Saunders Redding, and Joyce A. Joyce. Vol. 1. Washington, DC: Howard U P, 1991. 2 vols. 1991-92.

CHAPTER TWO

THE DEVELOPMENT OF SONIA SANCHEZ
A CONTINUING JOURNEY

Every literary period has its authors whose works defy easy, unambivalent categorization. The works of Black American writers usually rest at the heart of this rule. Much of the early criticism surrounding the Black poetry that began to flourish during the sixties shows how literary criticism tends to adjudge the merit of a new, innovative work or genre by using old preconceived notions that affix the work in the quagmire of tradition. Arthur P. Davis' essay "The New Poetry of Black Hate" exemplifies the misconceptions and misunderstanding that embody the Black poetry of the 1960s. He writes, "The newness, except for the hate motivation, is about as meaningful as the change from a 'konked head' to a 'bush'." (390) Professor Davis totally dismisses the relationship between the new Black poetry and the Black cultural and political milieu that characterizes the 1960s. Organizations like SNCC and CORE as well as such diverse Black political thinkers as Stokely Carmichael, H. Rap Brown, Julian Bond, Huey Newton, Medgers Evers, Martin Luther King Jr, Malcolm X, and Elijah Muhammad directed Black people toward a new consciousness that began to attack the political, economic, and social ramifications of slavery with a new force.

This intense period of political activity which included increased voter-registration drives, sit-ins, boycotts, and riots was accompanied by a change in the Black literary and cultural movements. Both the Black musician and the Black poet began to redefine themselves outside the context of the traditional Euro-American aesthetic framework. Leading the cultural break with the western-dominated tradition, the jazz musicians John Coltrane, Sonny Rollins, Ornette Coleman, Cecil Taylor, Pharaoh Sanders, and Sun Ra turned inside themselves, to their Black experiences, and to their Black past for the innovative aesthetic framework they gave to jazz. The new Black poets of the 1960s looked to these vanguards for the technical innovations and spiritual awakening they needed to inform their poetry. The 1960s then are characterized by a merger of the political and aesthetic movements whose goal is the spiritual liberation of Black Americans. The content and physical form of the Black poetry of the 1960s are outward and visible signs of a new consciousness, Black people's new eyes began to see how their "konked head" reflected their imitative relationship to the white society. The Black Power Movement, Stokely Carmichael's speeches, Malcolm X's speeches, John Coltrane's music, and the new Black poets repudiated this imitative relationship, emphasized the uniqueness of Black history, and stressed the Black community's need to withdraw from the malign influence of the Euro-American political, social, and aesthetic entrapments.

Sonia Sanchez remains one of the proudest and the most vibrant of those figures whose works manifest this spiritual link between art and politics. She teaches in the Pan-African Studies Department at Temple University and her six volumes of poetry beginning in 1969 with *Home Coming* have fallen prey to the misconceptions and neglect that encage the new Black poetry which began in the 1960s. The dearth of essays on Sonia Sanchez' craft as well as the simplistic and superficial reviews of her poetry testify to the lack of serious attention given to her "vitriolic verse." Although Sonia Sanchez is one of the most well-known names of the contemporary Black poets, the white feminist Dexter Fisher excludes Sanchez from her anthology *The Third Woman: Minority Women Writers of the United States* (1980), a work which includes the contemporary, well-known Lucille Clifton, Gwendolyn Brooks, Mari Evans, June Jordan, Audre Lorde, Ntozake Shange, Nikki Giovanni, and Margaret Walker. Sanchez' absence is too conspicuous to overlook. Her poetry, perhaps, is the most nontraditional in form and the most derisive in content of all the poets in this group with the possible exception of Shange's works which belong to a later time period. The more a poet's technique varies from the norm of the White American literary tradition and the more the poet repudiates the American political, social, and racial status quo, the more she/he is dubbed a "revolutionary" and thus the less seriously the traditional American literary society takes their works. Although the Black poetry of the 1960s reflect the influence of nontraditional White writers like e.e. cummings, the young poets shunned the sonnet and many western poetic techniques. Their goal was not to show white American society that they were like them; instead their aim was to illuminate their uniqueness, their Blackness.

Their unique poetic innovations find their sources particularly in Black speech and Black music. Thus this new poetry is rooted in the Black experience, a communal experience. And the Euro-American critical tradition is not prepared to deal with an art form that shapes itself around the languages, customs, and desires of any community, particularly the Black community. Until Professors Mercer Cook and Stephen Henderson's *The Militant Black Writer* (1969), not much had been written to define the aesthetics of this new Black poetry by a critic who was not essentially a poet himself. The poets Don L. Lee, Carolyn Rodgers,

Sarah Fabio Webster, and W. Keorapetse Kgositsile had all
expressed their views toward the new Black poet and
her/his art in a series of essays which appeared in the
Negro Digest from September 1968 through November
1969. This series of essays, *The Militant Black Writer*, and
Henderson's later, invaluable *Understanding the New Black
Poetry* (1972) mark the beginnings of the Black literary critics' attempts to pull the new Black poetry out of the quagmire of obscurity and denigration imposed upon it by
white literary and cultural traditions.

   If we are to appreciate Sonia Sanchez' poetry, we must
wash away all Euro-American, middle-class notions of
what can and cannot be said in poetry and even of how a
poem should look on the printed page. Abrasively strong
in content and challenging in form, Sonia Sanchez' poetry
addresses itself to the Black community. Her concerns and
the development of her thought conform to Don L. Lee's
definition of the Black poet. Lee says:

> The images and symbols that are used will come
> out of the poet's immediate surroundings and
> will accent his particular lifestyle. This means
> that black poets will deal with themselves as
> "individuals" first and then will move toward a
> concept of "peoplehood"; better yet, they will
> move from the *I* to the *we* to the *us* and the *our*.
> The black poet, is at *all times*, in tune with his
> people; he is an integral part of the black com-
> munity; a guiding force; a walking example as
> opposed to a walking contradiction. Black, for
> the black poet, is a way of life. (Lee 27-8)

   Before tracing the development of Sanchez' poetry by
analyzing specific, representative poems I would like to
augment the critique of her poetry with a theoretical discussion of how her poetry reflects the steps in an artistic
consciousness that moves from extreme subjectivity to a

communal peoplehood to an objective perspective to an acquiesced, collective psyche. This creative process is precipitated by the tension in her poetry between simplicity and depth as well as spirituality and rationality.

Her first volume *Home Coming*, published by Broadside Press, contains a number of what Carolyn Rodgers refers to as "bein poems." In these poems Sanchez writes about "the way she be, her friends be, her lovers be, and the world be." (Rodgers 12) This early poetry is stylistically unintellectual, unacademic, and anti-middle-class, for her idioms come straight from the mouths of those Black people who intuitively understand that vulgarities cut deeper and closer to our real feelings than do the niceties of standard middle-class English. Hence her use of obscenities make up an integral part of her political statement. Her second volume of poetry *We a BaddDDD People*, also published by Broadside in 1970, is a more extensive volume than the earlier *Home Coming*. *We a BaddDDD People* remains perhaps the strongest of Sanchez' verse. Also containing several "bein" poems, this volume more clearly coalesces Sanchez' repudiation of all the evils that beset the Black community. She attacks pimps, drugs, prostitutes, television, policemen, and "white brainwashing," which keep Black people from loving themselves, from being themselves, and which has stunted healthy relationships between Black men and Black women. This volume marks a progression in her step toward "peoplehood." She moves from the subjective singular *I* to the subjective plural *we*. Another major concern throughout her canon is the future of Black children. Her third book of poetry published in 1971, *It's a New Day*, is subtitled "poems for young brothas and sistuhs." Her objective stage begins here. For our children represent *us*. If we look into their eyes, we see ourselves. They are the *objects* that serve as the medium through which Sanchez guides Black people. In this volume she teaches Black children to love themselves, to be proud of their African heritage. She particularly addresses young Black men, attempting to instill self-esteem in them by explaining that they are descendants of Black warriors.

Up to this point (from 1969 to 1971) Sanchez' themes and style show little change. But with her fourth volume of poetry, *Love Poems*, published in 1973, she begins to modify her craft and her Islamic ideology more overtly infuses her thought. Still using an image or language that roots her in her Black experience, she now begins to write Haiku poetry whose subject matter is love and lovemaking or the relationship between Black men and Black women, the Black father and his African heritage, and the social conditions that stifle Black peoples' lives. Her images come directly from nature and the Black communal environment. These Haiku poems and the relaxed style of the other poems in this volume presage the mellowed style of her next two volumes, *Blues Book for Blue Black Magical Women* (1974) and *I've Been a Woman* (1978). *Love Poems* brings Sanchez to the final stage in the move from the *I* to the *we* and to the *us* to the *our* in her role as a "guiding force" in the Black community. She moves from an objective perspective back to a plural subjective stage. In *We a BaddDDD People* she tells Black people that they should love themselves, that they should deal with themselves, and that they should know what they are about. And in *Love Poems* she shows how this knowledge serves as the basis of a healthy relationship between Black men and Black women and how the lack of it causes pain and disappointment. Her poetry metaphorically exemplifies the contradictory traits that embody love. While love requires self-control and self-discipline, it also stimulates the lover's desire to control or to dominate. But before the lover is worthy of controlling others, he must understand and control himself. The progression of Sanchez' canon demonstrates her search for self-knowledge.

Her next volume of poems, *Blues Book for Blue Black*

Magical Women, is a journey that returns to the subjective *I* and moves to the possessive *our* by tracing the development of her emotional growth as a Black woman and as a poet. This autobiographical, spiritual, meditative journey shows how the author came to terms with dealing with herself as she grew in her awareness of her Black womanhood and in her relationship to the world around her. Reflecting the mystical aura that imbues *Blues Book*, the style in this collection depends heavily on figurative language and ritual to convey meaning. Still open and sensual, *Blues Book* illuminates Sanchez' change in relationship to the world around her. The Black speech that she applauds in her earlier poetry and her overt political statements become infused with images and metaphors and this change is even more pronounced in *I've Been a Woman*. By 1978 she relaxes her vituperative style that was so characteristic of her earlier poetry. We do not need to be aware of the poet's separation from her husband Etheridge Knight (who is the subject of many of her early poems) nor of other soul-searching times in her life to see the effect time has had on her craft. By the time she reaches *Blues Book* and *I've Been a Woman*, she begins to feel the inside of things. No longer working on the outside as spokeswoman, she relies on language, using similies and metaphors which suggest a spirit that infuses the peoples of the East and all people of Eastern heritage. This spirit subdues the anger that pervades her early poetry. Anger no longer possesses her; she possesses it.

In order to trace the dissolution of this anger and the growth of the spirituality in Sanchez' poetry, I choose to concentrate on five of perhaps the most predominant themes that suffuse her poetic canon. The most common of these in *Home Coming* and *We a BaddDDD People* is the "bein" poem, the poem that emphasizes the self and how this self sees the world around it. The title poem "Homecoming" of her first volume puts the self at the cen-

ter of the poem and concentrates on the poet's immediate
response to her environment after she returns from her stay
at college. The opening section of the poem introduces the
stylistic characteristics and the concerns peculiar to
Sanchez' first volumes:

> i have been a
> way so long
> once after college
> i returned tourist
> style to watch all
> the niggers killing
> themselves with
> three for oners
> with
> needles
> that
> cd
> not support
> their stutters. (*Home Coming 9*)

Her returning home "tourist style" suggests her role
as artist. Back among her people, she now has the vision
and perspective to make them conscious of the commercial
and societal evils that manipulate their lives. One of the
most exploitative commercial ploys is the advertisement
that beguiles us into thinking we have a bargain if we buy
three items we don't need for the price of one. Sanchez'
language here cautions Black people against getting caught
up in the tide of the American Dream which demands that
Americans surround themselves with useless material pos-
sessions. Because many Blacks find it impossible to achieve
the rewards of this dream, they seek solace for their frus-
trations and disappointments in drugs. Ironically, the same
forces that prevent them from sharing in the American
Dream are the same forces that profit from the sale of
drugs. As a result the drug users are a part of the network

that makes the rewards of the dream possible for others. These users kill themselves "with needles that cd not support their stutters."

The poet's language comes out of her immediate surroundings and accents the people's lifestyle, as exemplified by the word *stutter*, which appears quite frequently in her poetry. She uses *stutter* both literally and figuratively. While drug users often stutter from the physical effect of heroin, they also fill their lives with hesitations, with prolongations; for they cannot move beyond their dependence on drugs to a wholesome, straightforward, active attack of the evils that beset their lives and their community. And one of the most common words that are a part of the language of the Black community is *nigger*. While the Black middle-class fights desperately to keep the word out of their mouths and homes, the poets of the 1960s use the word as a weapon against all those middle-class ideas— social, political, and aesthetic imposed on the Black community by the American hegemony. Also a part of the language of the community is the synecdoche Sanchez uses to refer to whites in this next section of the poem:

> i have returned
> leaving behind me
> all those hide and
> seek faces peeling
> with freudian dreams
> this is for real (p. 9)

Substituting a part of the whole for the whole itself, these lines use "faces" to refer to the middle-class white society. Hide-and-Seek is a children's game which the poet uses to satirize the fanciful, pretentiously dramatic character of a white society that relies on Freudian psychology to complement its knowledge of reality. Like in the children's game, the adults search for what hides from them. They peel layer upon layer of their dream lives, seeking waking

realities. The Black community that the poet sees is "for
real." Each moment is a waking reality that confronts those
lives that make up the community about which the poet
writes.

In "a needed poem for my salvation," a paradigm of
the "bein" poem from *We a BaddDDD People*, the poet stresses her need to remove herself from the demands of the
Black community in order to rediscover and reinforce her
knowledge of herself. She begins by enumerating all those
outside the self whom she has taken seriously, including
"parents, school, children, friends, poets, the cracker,
day/time/nite/time rhetoric, lovers of slick/blk/rappin,
pimps and jivers." Sanchez writes this poem to and for herself. Its theme is the poet's desire to know herself, to love
herself, and to have confidence in herself. She ends with a
strong sense of her goal:

> git a phd in soniasanchezism.
> & dare any mother/fucka
> > to be an authority on
> me.
> (cuz i'll be wounded with sonia/learnen/
> beauty/love and will be dangerous)
> > > yeh. all
> things considered.
> > gonna be serious about
> mrrrrrr and livvvve.
> (*We A BaddDDD People* 50)

The stylistic techniques in this poem and in "homecoming" as well as their thematic concerns embody the
matrices of Sanchez' early work. Her refusal to use standard, academic English and her concomitant embracing of
the Black street idiom are a part of a political statement
which understands how language too is used as a form of
oppression. By refusing to use the language of the oppres-
sor, Sanchez strengthens her attack of white society and re-

affirms her affinity with and understanding of the problems that beset the Black community. The arrangement of
these poems defies all rules of traditional, Euro-American
aesthetics. Like her ex-husband Etheridge Knight, Sanchez
frequently uses the slash to emphasize the rhythm of a
poem and consequently how it should be read. We cannot
read a poem by Sanchez with the same inflections and
steady, quiet tonal quality with which we read Shakespeare
or Eliot. Her spelling of "BaddDDD" in "We a BaddDDD
People" and "meeeeee" and "livvvvve" in "a/needed/poem
for my salvation" indicates the energy and depth of feeling
that characterize Black speech. Her use of "motha/fucka"
and "soniasanchezism" also embodies Black speech.
"Motherfucker" has almost as wide a range of meaning in
the Black street idiom as "nigger." Through the speaker's
intonation alone, those in the Black community know
whether a woman is jubilantly aggrandizing her man or
angrily damning him when she calls him a "mothafucker"
or "nigger." Similarly, the rhythm of "soniasanchezism"
reflects cryptic Black speech.

Sanchez' stylistic repudiation of the Euro-American
poetic tradition complements her major thematic concern—the liberation of her people. Her subject matter is
aimed at teaching the people to know themselves, to be
self-reliant, and to enhance their awareness of their
exploitative relationship to the dominant American society.
Even in her "bein" poems her goal is to teach the people.
Thus in addition to these poems that place the self at the
center is Sanchez' larger concern of uniting Black people, of
making them trust the Blackness within themselves and in
each other. Major components of the theme of liberation,
the two most obvious reoccurring thematic threads in her
poetry are her attack of the political and societal evils that
attempt to demean the Black man's self-esteem and dignity
and her demonstration of the relationship between Black
men and Black women. She realizes that before Black peo-

ple can know who they are they must first understand
where they came from. Consequently, her use of Black
political figures, literary artists, and jazz entertainers as the
subject of poems both reinforces Black Americans' pride
and raises their racial consciousness.

In most of these consciousness-raising poems Sanchez
subordinates the *I*, the self as writer. She moves toward a
plural perspective in which the *I* becomes *we*, indicating
that she too is just a part of what she describes. One of the
most anthologized of these "teachin" poems from her first
volume is "to blk/record buyers." In this poem she specifically attacks the Righteous Brothers for their exploitative
aping of a style which originated with Black performers
like James Brown. Punning on "righteous," she explains,
"white people/ain't rt bout nothing/no mo." These lines
suggest that white people ironically attempt to internalize
and use to their advantage the same characteristics which
they belittle in Black people. She alludes to the Young
Rascals' hit "Grooving on a Sunday Afternoon," an imita-
tion of the Black popular style of the 1960s. Instead of
"grooving on a Sunday afternoon," Black people, the poet
explains, are either "making out/signifying/drinking/making
molotov cocktails/stealing" or "taking their goods from the
honkey thieves who ain't hung up on no pacifist jesus."
What appears here to be a simple list of the activities in the
Black urban community contains over three hundred years
of Black history. Brought to America as slaves Blacks were
forced to live emotionally, intellectually, and geographical-
ly stifling, inhuman lives. These impediments to a wholesome, free existence still persist long after slavery. Sex
(making out), language and retorts (signifying), drinking,
mocking war materials (making molotov cocktails), crime
(stealing), and religion (a pacifist jesus) are the placeboes
Blacks have used to assuage their pain. Music, of course,
continues to be the deepest expression of this pain and the
most sincere reflection of Black pride. Hence the poet asks

her readers not to listen to the artificiality of white musicians who ape them:

> play blksongs
>> to drown out the
> shit/screams of honkies. (p. 26)

And characteristic of the new Black poets of the 1960s who adapted their poetry to the rhythm and language of Black music, Sanchez ends with an "AAAH, AAAH, AAAH, yeah," which both emotionally affirms her point and aesthetically echoes the style of popular performing artists like Aretha Franklin and James Brown.

To Sanchez and other Black poets who began writing in the 1960s, jazz because of its improvisational style replaced both the blues form and the popular song as the quintessential medium that reflects the unique Black identity and need to change environments. Sanchez goes so far as to repudiate the blues. In "for my lady" and in "liberation poem," she condemns what she believes to be the submissiveness embodied in the sadness expressed by blues songs— "sounds of oppression," "struggle," and "strangulation," which result from the inability of Blacks to subdue their foe. She concludes that Black people must transform the hope expressed in the blues songs into revolutionary action. The final section of "liberation/poem" captures the beauty of Sanchez' technique by using the titles of blues songs to demonstrate the poet's message:

> no more
> blue/trains running on this track
>> they all been de/railed.
> am i blue?
>> sweet/baby/blue/
>>> billie.
>> no. i'm blk/
>>> & ready. (p. 54)

Sanchez alludes to "A Train" and Billie Holiday's "Am I Blue?" to suggest metaphorically the need for a new racial consciousness. This sharpened racial awareness will replace the blue (sadness, submissiveness) with the black (a ready, willingness to act). The poet asks that a new consciousness derail the blue train of the underground railroad and move Black Americans above ground to fight today's psychological and political problems. Sanchez' condemnation of the blues here is too extreme. As the late Larry Neal explains, the blues singer provides the pathway back to the Black spiritual past and functions as the historian, the voice of the Black community, and the shaper of morality, within this community. The blues songs then embody the "living folklore"—the myths, the aspirations, the pain, and the hope—of the, Black culture. Perhaps Sanchez' desire to move Black people beyond the psychological associations of slavery is responsible for her rejection of this art form securely rooted in the chattel history of Black people.

Manifesting the poet's knowledge of the complexities embodied in psychological and political infirmities, the thematic range in *We a BaddDDD People* exceeds that of Sanchez' first volume. While the "bein" poem predominates in *Home Coming,* Sanchez broadens her scope by subordinating the self to include a more collective, external focus on peoplehood in *We a BaddDDD People.* Some of these diverse subjects which will not be discussed here include a poem about Malcolm X, a historical poem inspired by Coltrane, a poem for Nina Simone, a poem inspired by Elijah Muhammad, a wedding poem, and a poem about the poetic art itself. More so than any other volume of Sanchez' poetry, this second volume captures the heart of the Black Arts Movement as well as the political environment of the 1960s. Perhaps the most influential medium through which the mass of Black people see each other and view the world outside their community is the

television. Appropriately then *We a BaddDDD People* contains three poems concerned with how television shapes
Black minds: "television poem,"summer/time T.V./ (is
witer than ever)" and "on watching a world series game."

Although all three poems share the goal of illuminat-
ing the political realities that effect the Black community in
the turbulent 1960s, Sanchez drives her points home best in
"summer/time T.V." She uses Black entertainers to show
why the Black community should not view Black middle-
class assimilationists as role models. An effective, caustic,
satirist, Sanchez assails Little Anthony and the Imperials,
Diana Ross, and Barbara McNair with lyrics from their
own songs. She heightens her condemnation with a kind of
mock dialogue in which the poem's persona "signifies" in
what superficially appears to be an aside or an after-
thought inside of parenthesis. But as the poem progresses,
the reader soon sees that these parenthetical, sarcastic
phrases contain the heart of the poet's message.

Perhaps, a look at the poem will illustrate my points.
It begins:

> little anthony
> > and the imperials
> singen
> > > (without jewish accents)
> > exodus
>
> > > "This land
> > > is mine.
> > > until i
> > > die this
> > > land is mine."
> > > > i'm hip
> > > > > cuz the whole/
> > fucken/place
> > > is up for grabs
> > > > and bloods be
> > singen bout die/en for

what ain't even theirs
(never can be
without fighten). (p. 30)

Alluding to the Vietnam war, Sanchez wittily highlights the irony and delusions behind the idea that Black
Americans should think of America as a home for which
they should die. The parenthetical asides strike at the core
of Little Anthony's careless lyrics. From Crispus Attucks to
the Vietnam War veterans, Black people have died for a
land that refuses to recognize them as human beings. Not
until Black people fight for their rightful share of land will
they be able to claim America as their own. The allusion to
Jews suggests the difference between the history of
American Jews and Black people. Although both are dis-
placed from their original homeland, the Black man alone
remains dispossessed.

Diana Ross and Barbara McNair present the same
kind of glittery, deluding message as Little Anthony.
Sanchez captures Ross' frivolousness and integrationist
lifestyle in the line,

diana
blowen back the soft/straight/strains
of her pressed mind. (p. 30)

These lines, of course, call to mind the image of the konked
hair style popular in the forties and 1950s, which represents
many Blacks' shame of their own coarse hair and their
desire to look like white people. In her early poetry,
Sanchez sometimes uses a traditional poetic technique to
call attention to her object of attack as she does in the allit-
erative line "soft/straight/strains." Ross pressed hair
reflects a "pressed mind" that refuses to identify with the
roots of its Black heritage. Ross and McNair even choose to
see themselves through the eyes of white America. Love
songs like Ross' "Baby Love" contain only a "remnant" of

Black suffering and are far removed from awakening a racial awareness in Black people. McNair even goes so far as to pose for *Playboy*. Neither she nor Ross adapts to the role that is needed of Black women. While Ross sings of submissive, oppressive, humble love, McNair's voice washes away all signs of her Black background. Both women's words and lifestyle reflect their failures as Black role models.

Little Anthony's, Ross,' and McNair's song titles become an essential element of the typography of the poem and function as part of the poet's attack on the Euro-American values that the entertainers emulate. This poem is one of Sanchez' most impressive typographical innovations. Her uneven polyrhythmic lines capture the flexibility and fluidity of Black speech and give the poem a real, living, vibrant quality. She writes a poem for Black people. And her language and the humor it evokes are typically Black. She continuously rejects the traditional Euro-American stanzaic form, use of capital letters, and traditional syntax. Sanchez spells her words the way they should be read. For example, the *ing* of verbs become en as in "singen," "fucken," and "die en." This *en* suffix is more guttural and explosive than the *ing* sound. Moreover, the slashes also enrich the polyrhythmic motor of the poem as exemplified by the final lines:

> and all of this
> happened in Amurica
> in the yr/of/
> tele/vised
> ass/asi/nations.
> 1968. (p. 32)

The slashes emphasize a pause that gives the poem an abrupt, vigorous, irregular rhythmic quality. The spelling of America ("Amurica") accompanies the year 1968 in dating the poem. "Amurica" mocks Lyndon Johnson's pronunciation of this word. Johnson, who became president after John Kennedy's assassination in 1963, was still president in 1968 when both Dr. Martin L. King and Robert Kennedy were assassinated.

The ending brings the poem full circle: it ends where it begins. For "televised ass/asi/nations" echoes the title, which is an ironic understatement that contains layers of meaning that surface in the final lines of the poem. Just as the Black viewing audience learns of Sirhan Sirhan's shooting Robert Kennedy and James Earl Ray's shooting Dr. King by watching television, the audience also sees itself belittled through the actions and eyes of Little Anthony, Ross, and McNair. Thus assassination and death in the poem are associated with the lack of leadership in the Black community. The Black entertainers' loss of soul and commitment to the Black community is a kind of death that stifles the psychological liberation of Black Americans. This entrapment broadens in scope in its relationship to the national political network that can televise an assassination it cannot prevent. Hence "summer/time T.V." is "witer than ever" because those Blacks whom the people look to for guidance fail to keep the community abreast of the political realities that control Black lives. Too many Blacks like Little Anthony, Ross and McNair still desire to become a part of a sterile, violent culture that only uses them as pawns and assassins.

Much more can be said about this poem. It is one of Sonia Sanchez' finest pieces and nicely represents the style and subject matter of her earlier works. Her voice in this poem and others like it is much like the voice of the Black storyteller in Zora Hurston's folktales. We have a Black person who mocks white society by imitating the tone of voice of a white person. Part of the humor rests in the interplay between the affected white dialect and the intruding Black speech. Sometimes Sanchez' change in voice or in her use of persona is quite subtle. An interesting discussion would result from a comparison of the personas in "221-1424 (San/francisco/suicide/number)" and "summer/time T.V." The jocose voice in "San/francisco/suicide/number" and the sardonic persona in "summer/time T.V." attest to the versatility of Sanchez' skill. And the subtlety and complexity of "summer/time T.V." and the diversity of the objects of attack in We a BaddDDD People make this volume Sanchez' strongest collection of poetry.

The diversity of Sanchez' subject matter reflects the depth and progression of her thought with each new volume of poetry exemplifying a mind in transition. Two of the more dominant concerns that take shape throughout her canon are her interest in the relationship between Black men and Black women and her interest in Black children. Two volumes of her work are written specifically for the young: the 1971 collection of poetry, It's a New Day (poems for young brothas and sistuhs) and the more recent 1980 collection of short stories, A Sound Investment. The message in these works coincides with Sanchez' consistent purpose from Home Coming and We a BaddDDD People to Blues Book and I've Been a Woman: to teach Black people to know themselves, to be themselves, and to love themselves. Only her style and the influence on her thought differ in these works written for young Blacks. By the time of the publication of It's a New Day in 1971, Sanchez had become a member of Elijah Muhammad's Muslim community. Her Islamic ideology infuses It's a New Day and Blues Book, her important fifth book of poetry. The introduction of Islam into her poetry is much like, yet smoother than Richard Wright's use of existential doctrine in his fiction. Just as the early Bigger Thomas is no less an existential figure than Cross Damon, Wright's existential outsider, Sanchez espouses much the same philosophy in It's a New Day as she did in the works that precede her obvious conversion to Islam. And interestingly enough, by the time she gets to I've Been a Woman (1978) and A Sound Investment, her Islamic doctrine becomes diffused by a broader Pan-African world-view.

It seems natural to suppose that Sanchez' readings in Islamic doctrine and her own search for the history of Black peoples led the way to her Pan-African ideology. In both the Islamic and African communities the family is an essential element of the larger community. And, of course, children form the basis of the family. *It's a New Day* addresses the problems in the Black community that impede the psychological development of the children who make up the core of the Black family and who will become the Black mothers, fathers, and political leaders of the future. Sanchez realizes that reinforcement is the most effective method of teaching. Thus if young Blacks learn to love themselves and respect their African heritage and if they are taught early to recognize and shun the psychologically crippling elements of the American culture, they will be strong, adult Black men and women. In "Safari," a representative poem from this collection, the poet uses metaphors from an African landscape to emphasize the young adults' African heritage and to sustain the attention of young minds:

> C mon yall
>> on a safari
> into our plantation/jungle/minds
> and let us catch the nigger
> roamen inside of us.
>> let us hang
>> our white aping
>> actions
>> on walls
>> with signs that
>> announce the last
>> of our nigger thoughts
>> is dead.
>> only blackness

> runs in our veins.
> Cmon yall
>> follow me on a new african safari
>> and Live! (It's a New Day 21)

Like many of Sanchez' poems, this poem progresses through a sustained metaphor. The African safari becomes a psychological, mind-opening journey for the Black youth. Through learning of his African heritage, the Black youth will be able to catch the "nigger" inside of him made by slavery and racism and destroy him.

A part of this process requires that Black people annihilate the image of God given to them by a Euro-American Christian tradition. In the middle section of the poem the poet calls to mind the picture of the last supper that hangs on the walls of many Black American homes. Instead of hanging the picture of a white Christ on the walls of his home, the Black man must slough off his mocking (aping) of the attitude, beliefs, and actions of the American hegemony. Ironically, he must replace the picture of Christ with his "white aping actions" and with signs that announce the death of a Black man who sees himself only through the eyes of white society. Just as the last supper marked the impeding death of Christ who died to redeem mankind (in the Euro-American Christian tradition), so will the "new african safari" awaken a consciousness in Black people that will give him new life, self-respect, and self-knowledge.

"Safari" is not typical of other poems in this volume. Its metaphysical conceit is perhaps too subtle for the very young. Nevertheless, their imaginations will capture the African landscape and in turn reinforce their affinity with Africa, fulfilling Sanchez' goal of making young adults curious of their history. She also lures the attention of her young readers by using repetition and rhyme in poems like "Don't Wanna Be" and the title poem "It's a New Day." "Don't Wanna Be" uses a refrain which introduces the

poet's repudiation of pimps, numbers manners, and
junkies respectively, all debilitating figures for the young to
emulate. The "new day" will have arrived when the youth
of today become the Farrakhans, Elijahs, Nyereres, Kings,
Gwendolyns, Sojourners, and Muslim women of tomor-
row. Sometimes the poet's references to Islam or Islamic
figures are sparse and at other times as in "We're not lear-
nen to be paper boys (for the young brothas who sell
Muhammad Speaks)," the ideology of the Black Muslims
forms the basis of the poem.

Stylistically *It's a New Day* marks a change in Sanchez'
poetry. Beginning with this third volume, the poet
removes the obscenity from her poetry. In an interview
conducted in 1977 by poet E. Ethelbert Miller for WHUR
Radio at Howard University, she explained that she wrote
It's a New Day for a group of students in New York who
told her that they were not allowed to read her poetry
because of its obscenity indigenous to Black speech, adding
that she "curses" in her poetry to achieve emphasis and to
get people interested in poetry, to pull them in. Alhough
she stresses her desire to "hurl obscenities at the obscene,"
she changes her tactics in her later works. (Interview)

Any mind that is as consistent with its devotion to the
educational and emotional well-being of the young as
Sanchez' would naturally be equally concerned with the
role Black women must play in society. Of course, this role
begins with the relationship of the mother to the child.
Sanchez stresses the need for Black women to love themselves and to love and respect their Black men. Again she
emphasizes that to love the self requires knowing the self.
Consequently, the Black man and woman must understand
how slavery and oppression have shaped their individual
attitudes toward the self and toward each other. Once they
understand how the ramifications of slavery have molded
their consciousnesses then they will be prepared to change
their children's destiny. This thematic thread—the relation-

ship between the Black man and his woman—undergoes a subtle change in the development of Sanchez' poetry. While *Home Coming* and *We a BadddDDD People* present a mundane, secular treatment of the feelings of the Black woman and her relationship to the Black man, *Love Poems* (1973) evinces clearly Sanchez' adoption of the principles of the Black Nation of Islam. This volume and especially the subsequent *A Blues Book For Blue Black Magical Women* make more evident the spiritual, mystical nature that embodies Sanchez' later works. This spiritual phase enriched by the teachings of Elijah Muhammad prefigures her broader embracing of the mythology, religion, and history of various Eastern cultures in the few new poems collected in *I've Been a Woman*.

Sanchez' interest in Eastern civilization and her increased number of love poems make her revolutionary character and messages more furtive in *Love Poems*, *Blues Book*, and *I've Been a Woman*. Because poems about love dominate in these works, Sanchez says that Amiri Baraka asks that she write more revolutionary poems that will educate Black people by making them more aware of racial realities. Sanchez, however, believes that love between Black people *is* a revolutionary activity. She says that she writes love poems so that Black people can understand the need to love each other. (Interview)

In addition to being known as a "revolutionary" poet, Sanchez has always been appreciated by many readers, particularly by women, as a love poet. In his introduction to *Home Coming*, Don L. Lee (Haki Madhubuti) ends by citing in full Sanchez' "short poem" about love as an example of how she strikes at the core of life, shunning "aesthetic dreams" and "fantasy." The poem reads,

> my old man
> tells me i'm
> so full of sweet

```
pussy he can
smell me coming.
maybe
        i
        shd
        bottle
        it
                and
sell it
when he goes. (p. 18)
```

By the time Sanchez gets to *Love Poems*, she overtly alters her approach, becoming significantly less bawdy though she remains just as pointed in her representation of her subject matter as she is here. Both *Home Coming* and *We a BaddDDD People* carry the seed of spirituality that comes to full fruition in *Blues Book* and *I've Been a Woman*. Yet the love poetry in these early works chants in a rough, vibrant, vernacular, polyrhythmic style.

Love Poems introduces Sanchez' Haiku poetry and thus highlights her growing interest in an affinity with Eastern cultures. This Japanese form enhances her ability to attack with wit and brevity. Echoing those earlier poems that treat the hurt the Black woman feels because of her problems with her man the following poem illuminates Sanchez' feel for precision and objectivity:

> if i had known, if
> i had known you, i would have
> left my love at home. *(Love Poems* 50)

On the surface Haiku poetry seems quite simple when in fact it is a rather difficult form to master. The form consists of three unrhymed lines that have five, seven, and five syllables respectively. According to the rules of the poetry contests in the Heian courts in Japan during the thirteenth century, wit and a playful air should be indigenous to the poem. Sanchez adopts the oriental form with natural ease. Instead of altering her personality and her style to satisfy this form, she adjusts the form to make it suitable for *her* technique. For instance, the restriction of the number of syllables on a line makes the poet's slashes unnecessary. Working inside this limitation, she uses word choice and the syllabic division of words to gain emphasis and to indicate the rhythm of a line. One of the most beautiful qualities of Sanchez' poetry is its gyrating rhythm. The position of the second *if* gives this poem a vigorous rhythmic quality characteristic of Sanchez' other poetry.

Her Haiku poems also reflect her sharpened use of a metaphor although her figurative language continues to be specific to the culture of the common individual. In one of these Haiku poems, a woman desires to break through the wall of reserve that separates her psyche from that of her Black man's:

> i could love you Black
> man if you'd let me walk in
> side you and become you. (p. 62)

Another poem written about the same time as this one uses the metaphor of a port where ships dock temporarily to address the instability and aloofness that characterize the Black woman's relationship with her Black man:

> your love was a port
> of call where many ships docked
> until morning came. (p. 61)

All three of the above poems are enriched by what Professor Stephen Henderson refers to as "saturation": "By 'saturation' in Black poetry, I mean several things, but chiefly (a) the communication of Blackness in a given situation and (b) a sense of fidelity to the observed and intuited truth of Black experience." Admittedly any reader

would be able to appreciate the sentiments expressed in
these poems, but the woman who lives the Black experience—who sees the pain her Black man feels when he is
unable to find suitable work, when his encounter with the
white establishment sends him home spent and embarrassed—envisions a sharpened, intense picture in her
imagination through association and memory.

The effects of slavery have hampered the Black man's
and Black woman's ability to cultivate the trust and stability that form the core of any love relationship. In the second
Haiku the woman asks to get inside her man's mind so that
she can see life through his experience and thus understand him, and in the third poem the poet refers to a relationship based merely on the sex act, one that ends with the
break of day because the man must again shield himself
from the psychological and financial blows hurled by the
white society. Sanchez in all her love poems attacks this
continuous cycle that stifles the love and trust Black people
should have for each other.

She is very bold and honest in her treatment of the
problems that face Black men and women. In *Home Coming*
and *We a BadddDDD People*, she includes several poems
that sardonically castigate the Black man's attraction to the
white woman and the white man's lust for the Black
woman. She asks for consistent racial solidarity. Her desire
for cohesiveness within the Black community and her
desire to enlighten the Black community of the evils of
middle-class white America made her a natural follower of
the teachings of Elijah Muhammad. An important aspect
of the Black Muslim religion is that the man fulfill his duty
as head of the family and that he and his mate raise their
children together by the ways of "Righteousness."
Moreover, racial solidarity forms the basis of Elijah
Muhammad's *Message to the Blackman*. Leader of the Black
Nation of Islam, Elijah Muhammad saw the white race as a
community of "devils" that have psychologically raped the

Black man of self-respect and love. The only way for the
Black man to begin to understand the depth of the feelings
of inferiority instilled in him by a racist society is to remove
himself from the cause of his malaise. Thus miscegenation
is also a manifestation of the evil which accompanies
racism. The Black man must protect his Black woman and
together they should seek knowledge of themselves.

"Poem No. 13" uses the concepts of Islam to demonstrate how the Black man and woman are two halves
whose love unifies them into a single whole. The style of
the poem is reminiscent of "summer time/T.V." and other
earlier poems where technique complements content.
Sanchez arranges the poem like a dramatic piece which
moves through a dialogue between a woman and a man.
The Muslim greeting "As-Salaam-Alaikum" and the
responding "Wa-Alaikum-Salaam" introduce the theory of
dependent opposites on which the poem is based.
According to the teachings of Elijah Muhammad, the Black
man is the original man and from him came all peoples.
Sanchez alludes to this idea in the lines:

> brother—and who moves my queen today?
> sister—my happiness creases the ground
>   as i walk my king. (p. 72)

The relationship between the Black man and his woman
should be one of interdependence with the man (the king)
serving as protector to his woman.

The sun and the moon, two of the three emblems that
represent the religion of the Nation of Islam, augment the
reciprocity that defines the relationship between the Black
man and the Black woman:

> brother—i have become the sun
> Sister—i feel your heat
> brother—it is hard for the sun to keep all the
>   light and not have a moon to give it to.

> sister—it is hard for a moon to deal
> without her sun. (p. 72)

According to the concepts of Islam, the sun and the moon represent freedom and justice respectively. (Muhammad 77) One cannot thrive without the other. The man needs the woman just as it is necessary that some object receives the light of the sun. Yet Sanchez' use of the sun and the moon has an even broader significance. In some Eskimo mythologies, the sun and the moon are both husband and wife as well as brother and sister. Consequently, the two halves are opposites that share the same origin like Osiris and Isis, the husband/wife, brother/sister god and goddess of ancient Egyptian mythology. Epithets that Muslims and other Blacks use to address each other, "brother" and "sister" in the poem refer indirectly to the common origin of Black peoples.

This origin becomes the entire subject of *A Blues Book for Blue Black Magical Women*. This work is not a collection of individual poems. Instead it is an autobiographical, spiritual, poetic, narrative chant. Not only is it Sanchez' most unusual work, but it also mockingly suggests the difference between Afro-American poetry and the prototype of Modern American poetry. An anonymous reviewer for *Choice*, a publication of the Association of College and Research libraries, totally fails to see the breadth and ingenuity embodied in *Blues Book*. The writer maintains:

> There is an honest effort by Sanchez in these poems to assert her identity as a black, as a female, as a Muslim, as a keeper of society. But there is a distinction between creative art and polemic statement: she has yet to face the choice between personal honesty and party line. The collection is to be read as a soul struggling to cope, perhaps, with too many burdens at once, and as such represents an emerging conscious-

> ness—as Africa emerges—about how to deal
> with multiple and confusing realities. (*Blues
> Book* 944-5)

This statement is only correct in its listing of the general
themes—the poet's identity as a Black, as a female, a
Muslim, as a political activist, and in its reference to an
emerging consciousness associated with Africa. Otherwise
the reviewer completely misses the aesthetic beauty that
indeed coalesces "creative art and polemic statement." This
union, of course, is not unique to Sanchez. Literary artists
from antiquity until very recently held this synthesis as
their goal. Interestingly enough, one of the most polemical
statements in modern poetry is T.S. Eliot's revered *The
Waste Land*, a meditative journey which treats the decline of
western civilization. The paradoxical thematic and stylistic
similarities between Eliot's *The Waste Land* and Sanchez'
Blues Book are strikingly obvious if the reader follows
Sanchez' carefully laid clues.

Because the reviewer for *Choice* approaches Sanchez'
work with a categorical, myopic eye, he fails to perceive the
unsuspecting affinities between the two works. Part of the
problem begins with the misconception that *Blues Book* is a
collection of poems. On the contrary, *Blues Book* takes the
reader on a quest that is divided into five parts. Like in
Eliot's *The Waste Land*—also divided into five parts—the
reading undertakes a journey in which he/she acquires
knowledge. Both her content and her stylistic allusions
suggest Sanchez' use of *The Waste Land*. Her reference to
Eliot's work, however, is ironic. In *The Waste Land*, Eliot
laments the decline of western civilization through what he
refers to as the "mythical method." A complex network of
symbolism, naturalistic imagery, and mythology, *The Waste
Land* is shaped by a cluster of allusions to art, literature,
and music. Eliot's reference to works of the past reflects
what he calls the "historical sense":

> ...the historical sense compels a man to write not
> merely with his own generation in his bones, but
> with feeling that the whole of the literature of
> Europe from Homer...has a simultaneous exis-
> tence and composes a simultaneous order...He
> must be aware that the mind of Europe...is a
> mind which changes, and that this change is a
> development which abandons nothing en route,
> which does not superannuate either Shakespeare, or
> Homer, or the rock drawing of the Magdalenian
> drauhtsmen. (*T. S. Eliot: Selected Essays* 4-6)

When Eliot traces the history of western civilization back to
Europe and then to Homer, he not only excludes Black
Americans, but he also totally ignores all of Eastern civilization, *more* than one half of the world. His "historical
sense" also exemplifies the significant difference between
the aesthetics and purpose of the Black poetry of the 1960s
and the poetry of the Euro-American tradition. Eliot
describes a stagnant tradition with a set of aesthetics that
excludes the community. The common individual, the
individual who is not an artist, is not a part of history
according to his definition. The Black poets of the 1960s
explored new aesthetic values whose goal was the spiritual, cultural, political awakening of the common man as
well as the artist. The Black Arts Movement sought to give
a total vision of man. Their scope and perspective include
and depend upon the history of the Eastern, ancient part of
the world which Eliot and the western tradition ignore.
Sanchez heightens her condemnation of the limitations
embodied in the western literary tradition by mocking the
style of the most highly praised poem in modern American
poetry.

    She uses Eliot's limitation to enrich her poetic presen-
tation of the history of Black people. This time her skill at
achieving a harmonious balance between form and content

reaches its peak. Like Eliot, she wishes to return to the beginning, to the past, to the beginning of things. Her particular subject is the Black woman, the mother of civilization. By adopting the stylistic techniques of *The Waste Land*, she suggestively repudiates Eliot's assumption that civilization begins with Europe and thus with what has become known as "classical times." *Blues Book* is an autobiographical journey whose content and style exemplify Black peoples' Eastern heritage. In this ingenious and highly unusual work, the poet furtively alters her earlier iconoclastic tactics. The casual reader, who misses the significance of the relationship between Eastern cultures and the belief held by the believers of the Black Nation of Islam, might find *Blues Book* an un-unified, burdensome task as the reviewer for *Choice* suggests. If we read the work as merely a prose sermon that expounds the major tenets of the Black Muslims (Williams), we lose most of its meaning. While Eliot incorporates myths that represent his past into *The Waste Land* to demonstrate the decline of western civilization, Sanchez refers to the myths of ancient Egypt and the concepts of the Nation of Islam to show that the Black woman is the mother of Eastern civilization. Her allusions to Eliot's work assail the idea that antiquity rests with the West and ironically undercut the paragon of modern American poetry.

She realizes that before the Black man is able to understand the present and prepare for the future, he must unearth his history, a past hidden by the dominance of a European tradition. Thus Sanchez' search for self-knowledge led her East to the beginning of life. With the knowledge acquired from this archetypal journey, she is reborn. Sanchez introduces her allusions to Eastern culture with an epigraph which is the most important sura in the *Holy Qu'ran*. This sura explains that the *Holy Qu'ran* contains the knowledge man needs for guidance. By placing the sura at the beginning of *Blues Book*, Sanchez too emphasizes her goal of teaching Black people:

> 1. *Read!*
>   *In the name*
>   *of thy Lord and Cherisher*
>   *who created...*
>
> 2. *Created man, out of*
>   *a clot...*
>
> 3. *Read! And thy Lord*
>   *is most bountiful...*
>
> 4. *Who taught*
>   *by the pen*
>
> 5. *Taught man that*
>   *which he knew not.* (*Blues Book* 9)

Both this epigraph and the passage from Petronius that introduces *The Waste Land* demonstrate their authors' use of different traditions. This sura begins the religious doctrine that infuses *Blues Book* and explains Sanchez' purpose—to enlighten her people.

She entitles the five parts "Introduction (Queens of the Universe)," "Past," "Present," "Rebirth," and "Future" respectively. The introduction is a monologue that speaks directly to Black women, enumerating the malignant aspects of the American culture, explaining how Black people (the Black women) must instigate their own change, emphasizing what must be done for Black children, outlining the essential role of the Black woman, and ending with an urge for Black people to organize in the Nation of Islam so that they can be reborn in Blackness. In order to be reborn they must know their past. The rest of the book traces the growth of the poet's consciousness. Parts two through five give personal examples of what happened to

one Black woman (whom I identify with the poet). Thus
the self and the general become one. Part two (entitled
"Past") opens with an invitation to the reader to accompa-
ny the poet on a journey. The language in this opening section echoes the journey of the African slaves to new land:

> Come into Black geography
> you, seated like Manzu's cardinal,
> come up through tongues
> multiplying memories
> and to avoid descent
> among wounds
> cruising like ships,
> climb into these sockets
> golden with brine. (p. 21)

Instead of our going westward, the poet asks that we trav-
el back through time moving eastward. The metaphor of
the ship suggests the Egyptian symbol of the woman as a
vessel:

> In the Egyptian system of heiroglyphs, a deter-
> minative sign corresponding to the idea of
> receptacles in general [it is the vessel]. It is a
> symbol whose immediate significance is that of
> the context in which the intermingling of forces
> takes place, giving rise to the material world.
> From this sense arises a secondary symbol-
> ism—that of the female matrix. (Ciriot 341)

The metaphor then alludes to the Black woman as the
mother of civilization.

Next the poet summons up her earth mother from
whose thighs the poet is born. In this mystical, spiritual
scene the coming of the earth mother is accompanied by
the ringing of bells. The bells associated with a spiritual figure are reminiscent of the bells that Muhammad heard as
Allah revealed himself to him through Muhammad's reve-

lations. Similarly bells announce the knowledge of the
poet's birth revealed by her earth mother. This short scene
consists of a quasi-dramatic interchange between the
"Black Girl (the poet) and her earth mother. From this section (birth of the young Black Girl), the poet moves to early
girlhood. Although one section follows the other in chrono-
logical order with a sparse narrative line, *Blues Book* moves
through a series of vignettes much like Eliot's *The Waste
Land*. And like T.S. Eliot, Sanchez alters the language in a
particular scene to have it parallel the subject matter as she
does at the beginning of this section:

> fivetenfifteentwenty
> twentyfivethirtythirtyfiveforty
> fortyfivefiftyfiftyfivesixty
> sixtyfiveseventy
> seventyfiveeighty
> eightyfieninety
> ninetyfiveonehundredreadyornothere i come.
>   (p.26)

This children's game referred to as Hide-and-Seek
emphasizes the mind of a child that controls this section
and the young girl's alienation from her father and step-
mother. The poet describes the young girl's life as lonely
and reserved. An italicized chant serves as a refrain that
repeats the thoughts of the young girl's mind. This insight
into her consciousness complements the game that opens
Part Two:

> *no matter what they do*
> *they won't find me*
> *no matter what they say*
> *i won't come out.* (p. 27)

She does come out into "young womanhood."
Her period of young womanhood is characterized by

love and the aping of white middle-class values. The poet
lists the activities of a young Black woman completely separated from her Black roots and her Black community.
Learning foreign words, wearing lipstick, going to parties
and bars, eating cheese and caviar, and drinking wine at
downtown village apartments make up the activities of a
young Black woman living a life that severs her from her
ancestral ties:

> and my name was
> without honor
> and i became a
> stranger at my birthright. (p. 32)

The young woman's link with her birthright begins with
three visions that she has during the night. Bodies without
hands, laughter without mouths, faces crawling on the
walls like giant spiders reached out to her, accusing her of
ignorance and sterility. Upset by these dreams, her man
takes the young woman to a psychiatrist whose "european
words" handcuffed her. After a month of living in her past,
the poet followed the voices of her ancestors and became
active in political activity. The violence and humiliation
that accompanied the picketing and sit-ins in the 1960s cat-
apulted her into a deeper awareness of a self that understands the relationship between the present Black generation and the ancestors who suffered first. The young
woman "vomited" up the past which contained "the stench
of good ship *Jesus* carrying Black bodies to a new world,
the memory of Dahomey, Arabia, Timbuktoo, Muhammad,
Asia, Allah, Denmark Vesey, and Nat Turner." This new
sense of Black history prepares the poet for the concepts of
the Nation of Islam.

In the next section subtitled "womanhood," the poet
becomes a follower of Elijah Muhammad. This brief section
weaves Elijah Muhammad's teachings into the fabric of the

poem. The poet calls herself "the eldest daughter of the womb/eldest daughter of the world," alluding to the idea of the Black man being the "original man" and to the concept of the earth mother, the feminine earth. Her assimilation of the ideas of the Nation of Islam is even clearer in these lines:

> and i called out to prophesy
> to make me a woman
> of the beginning tribe
> to make me a woman of
> tyrannical love to
> cover our wounds. (p. 38)

The beginning tribe is the tribe of Shabazz. According to Elijah Muhammad, Black people are the descendants of the Asian Black Nation and the tribe of Shabazz, the original tribe that came with the earth after an explosion divided this planet into the earth and the moon. This tribe was the first to populate the Nile Valley in Egypt and the Holy City of Mecca in Arabia. Because of the suffering embodied in the history of Black people, the poet asks that her love be "tyrannical" so that she will have the strength necessary to help heal the wounds of the Black community. "Womanhood" ends by using the position Muslims assume during prayer as a metaphor for the love that the Black man must feel for himself:

> and
> i gave the birth to myself,
> twice in one hour.
> i became like Maat.
> unalterable in my
> love of Black self and
> righteousness
> and I heard the
> trumpets of a new age

and i fell down
upon the earth
and became myself. (p. 39)

In the final stages of the Muslim prayer, the believer bows
prostrate and places his forehead, nose, and palm on the
ground. Prayer and the righteousness found in Islam reinforce the poet's love of herself. In a simile she compares the
steadfastness of her love to Maat, the Egyptian goddess of
righteousness. In the Egyptian Book of the Dead, Maat
means true, right, real, genuine, upright, steadfast, and
unalterable. (Budge cxix) Moreover, in his *Message to the
Blackman*, Elijah Muhammad consistently refers to Black
people as the "Righteous." By turning to the East—as
Muslims do in prayer—and to the truth and righteousness
of Islam—the Black man can achieve the knowledge that
will bring him self-respect and self-love.

Part Three entitled "Present" is a celebration of the
knowledge of the past and of the self acquired by the poet
who represents and speaks to Black women. She sings
praises to the ancient Black women and grandmothers who
are now embodied in her. Continuing her inverted use of
The Waste Land, Sanchez uses language that suggest fertility and procreation while Part Three of *The Waste Land* ("The
Fire Sermon") indirectly refers to sterility, debauchery, and
lust. In "The Fire Sermon" whose title in part implies a
burning of lust, Eliot alludes to Spenser's "Prothalamion,"
the hermaphroditic Tiresias, Queen Elizabeth and
Leicester, all serving as historical examples that characterize a time when love had meaning, when love led to transcendence. In the modern world, love and relationships
between men and women are sterile and love does not lead
to life, according to Eliot. He gives this section an enhanced
rhythmic effect in the repeated phrases.

Weialala leia

Wallala leialala. (*The Waste Land* 40)

He uses this chant-like phrase once to echo the sound of
water and again to mimic the peal of bells. Sanchez uses a
similar phrase that represents the singing of the
"ancient/black/woman":

hay-hay-hay-hay-ya-ya-ya
hay-hay-hay-hay-ya-ya-ya. (p. 42)

This ancient Black woman is the mother of Eastern civilization. The poet and all Black women of the "Present"
contain the history and legacy bequeathed to them by their
ancient mothers. A part of this legacy is procreation. Hence
this part is replete with allusions to fertility and fruition:

and i taste the
seasons of my birth. mangoes, papayas.
drink my woman/coconut/milks
stalk the ancient grandfathers
sipping on proud afternoons
walk with a song round my waist
tremble like a new/born child troubled
with new breaths.
    and my singing
becomes the only sound of a
blue/black/magical/woman. walking
womb ripe. walking. loud with mornings.
    walking.
making pilgrimage of herself. walking. (p. 42)

The naturalistic imagery here suggests life whereas Eliot
uses nature in an ironic way to symbolize sterility and a
lack of natural order.

The poet's knowledge of her link with her past instills
a hope and an awareness of her role as a Black woman to
proudly give meaning to her life in much the same way
that the singing of the woman in Wallace Stevens' "The Idea

of Order at Key West" gives meaning and order to the sea. The teachings of Elijah Muhammad bring order and a new meaning to the lives of Black people. Sanchez refers to his reign as the "sun age." The sun is associated with change and its light brings Black people out of darkness of the moon to knowledge. In ancient Egyptian religion the sun was the emblem in which God made himself. (Budge xci-xciii) A representative of God, Elijah Muhammad brings Black people into the sun age out of the darkness of the teachings of Western civilization. By the time, we get to Part Four entitled "Rebirth," the poet has become purified by the light of the sun, the teachings of Islam. "Rebirth" is full of allusions to the sea, which represents a vast body of potential form. A symbol of fertility, the sea gives form to what is potential in the womb:

> whatever is truth becomes known. nine
> months passed touching a bottomless sea.
> nine months i wondered amid waves
> that washed away thirty years of denial.
> nine months without stains.

> ....

> i became mother of sun. moon. star children. (pp.47-48)

The Black woman then contains the potential energy that gives form to the future of Black people. Within their children rest the freedom (sun), equality (moon), and justice (star) that must govern Black peoples' lives. Through their children Black women are reborn as the the title of this section indicates.

The birth of the Black child—"the Black redeemer star"—symbolizes the hope of the future. Part Five is aptly called "Future." At this point, the poet has completed a journey through "Black geography." This quest becomes a metaphor for Black American history. The stages of the

journey begin in the East with the ancient earth mother
who gives birth to the young black girl. This young girl
through time grew unconscious of the sea that symbolizes
her beginnings. The light of Islam removes the veil of
darkness from her past and instills a knowledge and a love
of self that becomes manifest in childbirth. Consequently,
in the child, the symbol of the future, lay the signs of the
Black man's beginning and his end. Part Five proposes the
idea that life is a constant state of becoming rather than
being. In order to emphasize this cyclic process and to
bring her theme and parallel structure full circle, Sanchez
alludes to *The Waste Land* again in the first section of Part
Five called "signs of the end" and to Eliot's *Four Quartets* in
the very last section called "in the beginning."

Part Five celebrates the reign of the spiritual. The
goals of the quest achieved, the poet must now return to
the community with her knowledge like Sir James Frazer's
Fisher King. "Signs of the end" demonstrates the unnatural
quality of the reign of "Black Darkness" that governed the
lives of Black people before the light of Elijah Muhammad:

> When the sun spins and rises in the West
> when the stars lose their boundaries
> when ancient animals walk together
> when the oceans recede
> when the drought bites the land
> without saliva
> when the earth is shredded like lettuce
> ....
> when the eye of Osiris becomes perfect
> when the day of uproar and pandemonium
>   begins
> when mountains fall like waterfalls
> when the fires circle the earth
> ....
> when the great wind carries all away
> when the great wind carries all away

Black Darkness. Blue Black Darkness. (p. 57)

Because the Egyptians thought the whole man and all his nine components were vital to an eternal life, they preserved the entire body after death. The physical form was equally as important as the spiritual form. Osiris, the god of resurrection, could never have a perfect eye because the Egyptian god is never totally separated from his physical, earthly form. Osiris' eye then is not perfect just as the sun does not rise in the West. Hence "signs of the end" uses naturalistic imagery to show the unnaturalness of the "Black Darkness" of western culture that shields Black people from their history.

Eliot alludes to the vegetation myth of the Fisher King to satirically attack the dryness and sterility of modern western civilization. In the modern world, "April is the cruelest month, breeding/Lilacs out of the dead land...." The land is dead and does not bring forth life as it does in Egyptian myths in which life (vegetation) grows from the buried bodies of the gods. Sanchez mocks Eliot's style, using his inversion of natural order of things to suggest the fall of western civilization for Black people and the rise of knowledge of the East. Section Four subtitled "hereafter" contains four visions that portend the reckoning of those Blacks who fail to live a life of truth and "righteousness" under the light of Islam, the destruction of whites, and the rewards of the righteous Blacks. A prayer reflects the rewards of the quest for knowledge. Whereas Sanchez begins *Blues Book* with a secular, mundane, rap-like "oath/poem to be said everyday" to help Black sisters, she places a sacred, prayerlike chant near the end of the volume to illuminate the spirituality of Muslim women and to illustrate the light of Islam in progress. Part Five affirms the light of Islam by ending with a tribute to Muslim women.

An allusion to Eliot's *Four Quartets* closes *Blues Book*.

Four Quartets represents Eliot's struggle to escape the sterility and hopelessness of *The Waste Land*. It is a spiritual journey in which the poet resolves that history lies inside the
individual and that a return to God is a return to self. For
mankind is committed to the natural order of things. In
"Burnt Norton," he writes,

> Time present and time past
> Are both perhaps present in time future
> and time future contained in time past.
>   (*Four Quartets* 13)

Although Eliot continues in a very abstract theoretical
manner, these lines suffice in our understanding of how his
message relates to *Blues Book*. Sanchez' central point is that
the Black woman must be purified in the knowledge of her
origins. Only after she knows her past will she be able to
understand the present. And she must understand that the
present becomes the past of the future. Consequently, the
future (the continuing end) finds its source in the beginning (the past).

Blues Book ends with this allusion to "East Coker," Part
Two of *Four Quartets*. Sanchez writes:

> In the beginning
> there was no end
> in the beginning
> there was no end
> in the beginning
> there was no end
> ·····································
> let us begin again the
> circle of Blackness
>   me and you
> ······························
>   you and me
> ····································
> & have no beginning

or endddDDDD! (pp. 59-62)

Again the style and spacing of the poem parallel the message. Because the Black woman is the "original man," her end is her beginning. If she follows a similar quest as the poet's, all signs will take her East to the beginning of civilization. Her end (self-knowledge) will lead to her beginning—Egypt and Arabia. The spacing and repetition of the lines "In the beginning/ there was no end" reflect this circular cycle.

Many of Sanchez' poems and certainly *Blues Book* contain layer upon layer of meanings. Yet to her audience— the community she returns to—her poetry from *Home Coming* to *Blues Book* is not arcane or heavily academic. A Muslim woman unfamiliar with *The Waste Land* would probably think my references to Eliot rather stitled. Despite the fact that *Blues Book* reads nicely as a quest into awareness that led the poet to the teachings of Elijah Muhammad, the allusions to Eliot enrich the reading of the poem and highlight Sanchez' subtle, keen wit that we have seen in earlier poems. Eliot writes about the decline of western civilization. Sanchez agrees with him; only she doesn't lament the decline. She celebrates it. While Eliot mourns the temporal aspect of love and seeks transcendence in art, Sanchez understands true transcendence for Black people is dependent upon their ability to love each other. This love begins in the relationship between the Black man and the Black woman. In order to destroy the malignant alienation that has impeded this love, Black people must seek self-knowledge through learning of their past, the first wholesome step of the love process.

Sanchez' technique and subject matter in *Blues Book* prepare us for *I've Been a Woman*. This volume is basically a selected collection of poems from her earlier volumes, excluding only *It's a New Day*, her children's volume. In addition to twenty pages of Haiku and Tanka poems, *I've*

Been a Woman contains six new poems collected under the subtitle "Generations." Although all of the new poems in one way or another demonstrate the continuum in the growth of the poet's consciousness, the last poem "Kwa mama zetua waliotuzaa" (for our mothers who gave us birth) best embodies the thematic threads of her earlier work and illuminates how old forms become new forms.

The first line of "kwa mama zetu waliotuzaa" is the same as the first line of the ending paragraph of Sanchez earlier play *SisterSon/ji*. This play which progresses solely through Sister Son/ji's monologue directly to an imagined listener identified with the audience presents the history of the twentieth-century Black woman. Her thoughts are an embodiment of her past. The play has a circular movement that begins with the old Mississippi woman and ends with her. The events in between are her enactment of her development or of her memories. Again knowledge is represented as the link between the past and the future. The line "Death is a five o'clock door forever changing time" indicates the consistency in the cycle of life. This line along with the title of the poem echoes the "In the beginning/there was no end" of *Blues Book*. Just as Sister Son/ji reaches out to the audience and asks if they will "grab the day and make it stop," "kwa mama zetu waliotuzaa" illustrates how the physical, temporal, historical reality becomes an embodiment of the spiritual. For if we grab the day and make it stop, we will see that death is a concrete reality (a five o'clock door) that rules the process of life. For the death of the natural world brings forth the birth of the spiritual (forever changing time) as Sister Son/ji learns.

"Kwa mama zetu waliotuzaa" is generally a poem that eulogizes the mothers of Black women. It specifically becomes an eulogy for Shirley Graham DuBois, the wife of W. E. B. DuBois. Before the reader learns that the poem is about Shirley Graham DuBois, the beginning passages set

up a theory of opposites that symbolizes the interrelationship between life and death:

> as morning is the same as nite death and life are
> > one
> spring. settling down on you like
> green dust. mother. ambushed by pain in
> rooms bloated with a century of cancer.
> yo/face a scattered cry from queequeg's wooden
> bier.
> > mother. i call out to you
> traveling up the congo. i am preparing a place
> for you. (*I've Been a Woman* 99)

Like the reciprocal relationship between morning and
night, the death of the temporal, physical body reflects the
reign of the spiritual. Thus the poet explains in reference to
Shirley DuBois and the other mothers who gave birth to the
Black woman:

> no longer full of pain may she walk
> ....
> abundant with lightning steps, may she walk
> abundant with green. trails, may she walk
> abundant with rainbows, may she walk
> as it was long ago, may she walk. (pp. 99-100)

In both the preceding quotations the poet uses naturalistic
and concrete images to suggest the natural quality of death
and the perennial presence of the spiritual. The reference
to the Congo and later allusions to Egypt, India, and China
function as general references to DuBois' travels in the East
and as a specific reference to her death in China. These references along with the Swahili title serve the same purpose
as the allusions to Egyptian mythology and the precepts of
Islam in *Blues Book*. They ground the poem in the East, in
the beginning of life for Black peoples.

Shirley Graham DuBois like Elijah Muhammad taught the poet the nature of her origins:

> in the center of death is birth
> in those days when amherst fertilized by
> black myths, rerouted the nile.
> you became the word (Shirley, graham, du bois
>   you were the dance
>   pyramidal sister
> you told us in what Egypt our feet
> were chained
> you. trained in the world's studio
> painted the day with palaces
> and before you marched the breath
> of our ancestors. (p. 100)

The knowledge gained through Shirley DuBois' journey through the East teaches the poet the true story of her ancestral roots. Hence the line "at the center of death is birth" carries a two-fold meaning: Shirley DuBois literally dies in China, in the East. She dies in the hemisphere of her birth place and her death becomes a part of the poet's spiritual awakening manifested in the writing of the poem. The effect of death upon the poet and her coming to terms with it is expressed in terms of a metaphor that exemplifies the change in Sanchez' style:

> i am circling new boundaries
> i have been trailing the ornamental
> songs of death (like a strong pine tree
> dancing in the wind
>
> i inhale the ancient black breath
> cry for every dying (living
> creature. (p. 101)

This metaphor of the strong pine tree symbolizes the reciprocal relationship between the strength of life and man's vulnerability to death. Death, however, is not to be feared. It is a natural process, like the seasonal change of nature in which the original need—the past—begins a new cycle that is embodied in the present, in the poet's consciousness.

Sanchez' earlier metaphors lack the suggestive, abstract quality of those in "kwa mama zetu waliotuzaa." In fact, this poem perfectly illustrates the change in the poet's technique. In the earlier pieces of *Home Coming* and *We a BaddDDD People*, she experiments with the spatial possibilities of the poem. Her typography enhances the polyrhythmic quality of the lines. This rhythm changes in "kwa mama," becoming more relaxed and thus much less staccato. Fewer slashes that once heightened rhythm and a subtle diffusion of Black speech also characterize the new poems in *I've Been a Woman*. And probably the most obvious change is the disappearance altogether of obscenities; this absence highlights Sanchez' mellowed tone. She continues to make her political statements though her new poems work more through suggestion and metaphor than through her earlier pointedness. Sanchez is still, however, as much a political activist as she ever was; only her form has changed. Her content still reflects her rooting herself in Blackness.

In *Home Coming* and *We a BadddDDD People*, she emphasizes in a mundane manner Black Americans' need to isolate themselves from the social, economic, and psychological evils of the Euro-American cultural tradition. And in *Love Poems* her Islamic ideology begins to lead Black men and women East for a true knowledge of what their lives should be about. Focusing on the ancestral heritage of the Black woman, *Blues Book* illustrates a consciousness that moves from ignorance to a knowledge of its beginning. The quest stimulated by the teachings of Elijah Muhammad led to a broader knowledge of Eastern civilization, manifested in "kwa mama zetu waliotuzaa" in *I've Been a Woman*. Sanchez' poetry is about spirituality. In an

essay entitled "On Spiritualism and the Revolutionary
Spirit," Ahmed A. Alhamisi presents an analysis of the revolutionary spirit that provides insight into the progression
of Sanchez' craft:

> ...a person writing about positiveness is not nec-
> essarily a spiritual person. But a spiritual person
> will almost always write spiritual things.
> Negativeness will disappear in his or her cre-
> ations; not out of necessity alone, but out of a
> more beautiful way, a natural way. It is a kind of
> refined simplicity, a re-beginning into what we
> were, what we are now...we must move to
> refelct the truth of our understanding an
> dkowledge in a more positive way; must become
> a living example of all we say and write.
> (Alhamisi 30)

Sanchez takes her knowledge of self and her awareness of history and shares them with the community. Her
first six volumes of poetry were published by Black press-
es. Thus despite this look inward that characterizes her last
works, we cannot say that she ceases to write with the goal
of edifying, uplifting us Black sisters and brothers. She has
come to terms with a stronger vision of self. Poems such as
"kwa mama zetu waliotuzaa" suggest that this vision
moves in a constant process of change.

WORKS CITED

Alhamisi, Ahmed A. *Black Art and Culture*. San Francisco: Journal of Black Poetry Press, 1972).

The Book of the Dead. Trans. E.A. Wallis Budge. 1895. New York: Routledge Chapman & Hall, 1969.

Ciriot, J.E. *A Dictionary of Symbols*. Trans. Jack Sage. New York: Philosophical Library, 1962.

Davis, Arthur P. "The New Poetry of Black Hate," *CLAJ*. 13 June 1970: 390.

Eliot, T.S. *T.S. Eliot: Selected Essays*. New York: Harcourt, Brace & Co., 1932.

_____. *The Waste Land and other Poems*. New York: Harcourt, Brace & World Inc, 1934.

_____. *Four Quartets*. New York: Harcourt, Brace & World Inc., 1943.

Lee, Don L. "Black Poetry: Which Direction." *Negro Digest*. Sept./Oct. 1968: 27-28.

Muhammad, Elijah. *Message to the Blackman*. Chicago: Muhammad's Temple No. 2, 1965.

Neal, Larry. "Black Art and Black Liberation." *The Black Revolution: An Ebony Special Issue*. Chicago: Johnson Publishing Company Inc., 1970.

Rodgers, Carolyn. "Black Poetry—Where It's At." *Negro Digest*. 18 September 1969: 12.

Sanchez, Sonia. *Home Coming*. Detroit: Broadside Press, 1969.

_____. *We a BaddDDD People*. Detroit: Broadside Press, 1970.

_____. *It's a New Day*. Detroit: Broadside Press, 1971.

_____. *Love Poems*. New York: The Third Press, 1973.

_____. *Blues Book for the Blue Black Magical Women*. Detroit: Broadside Press, 1974.

_____. Interview. WHUR, Washington, D.C. 20 March 1977.

_____. *I've Been a Woman*. Chicago: Third World, 1978.

Rev. of *Blues Book for Blue Black Magical Women*, by Sonia Sanchez. *Choice*. 2 Sept. 1974: 944-45.

Williams, Deborah. Rev. of *Blues Book for Blue Black Magical Women*, by Sonia Sanchez. *Library Journal*: 99 (1974).

CHAPTER THREE

THE CONTINUING JOURNEY OF SONIA SANCHEZ

FROM *HOMEGIRLS & HANDGRENADES* TO *WOUNDED IN THE HOUSE OF A FRIEND*

Sonia Sanchez' spiritual journey led to the publication of *homegirls & handgrenades* in 1984, *Under a Soprano Sky* in 1987, and *Wounded in the House of a Friend* in 1995. Although in a number of ways these three collections are strikingly different from each other, they share Sanchez' strong vision of the self and her desire to use that knowledge to awaken the spirit and heighten the political awareness of African-Americans—the community she engages most emphatically in her poetry. In his comprehensive examination of the life and works of Sonia Sanchez, Kalamu ya Salaam quotes the poet, explaining the purpose of her work:

> "The need to put work out that will help people
> hold on and survive, and to make people see a
> "win"
> or a hope, or a movement toward something, or
> even just
> some lines which say that yes "yes, the idea of
> freedom is still possible," or "I'm still moving
> toward
> that," or that struggle is a viable way of living--I
> think those are much more important kinds of
> things
> that need to be said." (306)

Akin to a long line of Caribbean, African, and African-American writers, such as Aime Cesaire, Leon Damas, George Lamming, Earl Lovelace, Leopold Senghor, Chinua Achebe, Ngugi wa' Thiong'o, Bessie Head, Frederick Douglass, Frances Harper, W. E. B. Du Bois, Langston Hughes, Margaret Walker, Richard Wright, and legions of others, Sanchez sees her art as communal. Her poems as well as her drama and essays reflect the commitment to use her art as a means of improving the well-being of Black lives throughout the world. In the tradition of Richard Wright, she sees the need to merge the roles of artist and political activist.

The style and content of Sanchez' poetry have their source in the African oral performance tradition. Although several books addressing the African oral performance have been published, Isidore Okpewho's seminal *African Oral Performance* provides the research that justifies grounding Sanchez' poetry within the African oral tradition. In fact, Okpewho's impressive study helps to clarify and place in context the work accomplished by the Black poets, including Sanchez, Larry Neal, Haki Madhubuti, Sarah Webster Fabio, Nikki Giovanni, Amiri Baraka, Askia Toure, and others who consciously and aggressively stressed the communal nature of their poetry, their connection with an African tradition, and their consequent stylistic and ideological separation from a European poetic tradition. According to Okpewho, traditional African societies used certain individuals to train the young in the study of various arts. In the absence of organized schools in traditional African society, ways of living and behaving were contained "in the various forms of oral literature practiced in the society—songs, narratives, proverbs, riddles, and so on—which are delivered either privately (e. g., mother to child, artist to apprentice) or publicly (e. g., in moonlight entertainment or in open performances by skilled artists)" (115).

Like traditional African oral literature, African-American literature, beginning with the slave narratives and the poetry of figures such as George Whitfield and Jupiter Hammon, grows out of Black peoples' lives and focuses on Black survival and well-being. Many of the African-American poets who began writing poetry in the 1960s strengthened their connection to an African aesthetic tradition, whereby their artistic productions are an integral aspect of their daily lives. Sanchez' poetry and that of her peers train the young and inform all Blacks of ways of living and behaving that will ensure their well-being and survival. Thus Sanchez' poetry provides the same service that Okpewho attributes to African oral literature. He also links the oral tradition to social identity: "A much wider service provided by oral literature is to give the society—whether isolated groups within it or the citizenry as a whole—a collective sense of who they are and to help them define or comprehend the world at large in terms both familiar and positive to them (110).

We scholars have failed to place Sanchez clearly and explicitly in an organized, codified, aesthetically intellectual African tradition because of the stereotype of African society as primitive. Despite numerous and diverse academic studies, including scholars Martin Bernal, Cheikh Anta Diop, Ivan van Sertima, Maulana Karenga, Molefi Asante, Isidore Okpewho, and Oyekan Owomoyela, the prevailing attitude toward Africa in the academy is that it is less sophisticated than Europe and America. In discussing the various translations of African oral literature by Europeans, Okpewho indirectly provides the reason why we have come late to an appreciation of the African oral tradition. In explaining how European translators attempted to force African oral poetry into European versification, Okpewho cites the following comment made by R. F. Burton, the author of the nineteenth-century text *Wit and Wisdom of West Africa*: "Poetry there is none....There is no

meter, or rhyme, nothing that interests or soothes the feelings, or arrests the passions" (294).

   Burton's comment is the precursor of twentieth-century American scholars, both Black and White, who dis-
miss the aesthetic value of much of the poetry written by
poets who comprise the Black Arts Movement. As I made
clear in the preceding essay, in order to appreciate the stylistic characteristics that came to dominate Black poetry
beginning in the 1960s, we cannot depend upon European
artistic tools to plumb the aesthetics of this poetry.
Particularly in Sanchez' case, a look at the technique of her
poetry leads us to the African oral tradition. While the
Euro-American poetic tradition finds its source in works
such as the *Aeneid, Beowulf*, and Chaucer's and
Shakespeare's poetry, Sonia Sanchez and other Black poets
have established a connection with an African artistic tradition with rules and standards that grow out of African
culture. In his explanation of the training and nurturing
environment provided the African artist, Okpewho emphasizes the technical skills the artist must learn to master:
"Whatever the environment in which artists find themselves, all of them are trained in fundamentally the same
skills: the sensitive use of words and images, the delicate
balance between music and words, the art of holding the
attention or interest of an audience, and so on" (29).

   While the traditional African artist (or griot) focused
on perfecting the oral performance, Sanchez masters the
technique of the oral performance as well as the art of transcribing that oral technique onto the written page. Striking
in appearance, artistically tight, forcefully effective,
Sanchez' poetry resembles a drama in its emotional content
and progression. The collections *homegirls & handgrenades,
Under a Soprano Sky*, and *Wounded in the House of a Friend*
reveal the poet's sustained interest in the complex effects of
drugs on the African-American community, the relationship between African-American men and women, the need

for every individual to know the self, the importance for African-Americans to be rooted in the knowledge of their history, the role of the artist as teacher, and the political entrapments aimed at stifling the economic, educational, and psychological vitality of African-Americans. While *homegirls & handgrenades* treats its themes aggressively, *Under a Soprano Sky*, as its title suggests, contains mature lyrical images. *Wounded in the House of a Friend* emerges as the poet's most sensitive collection. In this volume, Sanchez proves that poetry can be at once carefully crafted and emotionally challenging.

Always a priestess and warrior persistent in stressing the need for Black people to love each other, the poet subtitles the first part of *homegirls & handgrenades* "The Power of Love." Each of the four pieces and the two haiku in this section address in various ways the effect of love. "Poem No. 10" [also published in *Love Poems* (1973)] and the prose poem "Just Don't Never Give Up on Love" implicitly warn that the poet's busy lifestyle (which includes political activities) has sometimes diminished her capacity to see romantic love as an essential part of her life. "Poem No. 10" begins:

> You keep saying you were always there
> waiting for me to see you.
> you said that once
> on the wings of a pale green butterfly
> you rode across san francisco's hills
> and touched my hair as I caressed
> a child called militancy
> you keep saying you were always there. (3)

The image in the poem of a lover riding the wings of a "pale green butterfly" suggests the gentleness of a lover who perceives that the poet does not see him, but who understands that he must be patient as he waits for her to look up from her political struggles and recognize that he has always been "there."

When they move from San Franciso to Indiana, the poet finally notices with new eyes the man at her side:

> and you grew a black mountain
> of curves and I turned
> and became soft again. (3)

The three lines illuminate the brevity that is particularly characteristic of Sanchez' later poetry. The man, who was younger when he and the poet were in San Francisco, has now grown older, and she, having achieved some distance from the pain of previous love relationships, becomes soft again, opens her heart to the man who has waited for her to acknowledge his love. In the final stanza of the poem, the poet plays with time and space, which she sees simultaneously as separate and contemporaneous:

> you keep saying you were always there
> you keep saying you were always there
>   will you stay love
>   now that I am here? (3)

Style and meaning parallel, the typography of the above lines suggests the contemporaneity of past and present, manifested in the lover's continued presence in the poet's militant life and in her current recognition of that dedicated presence. Thus the sing-song, rhythmic journey in the poem is finally complete.

An excerpt in Spanish written under the subtitle of this first section of the collection, "un corazon solitario/ no es un corazon," from Antonio Machado, an author of the Spanish Civil War, warns the poet and the reader that a solitary heart is not a complete heart. The old woman in "Just Don't Never Give Up on Love" intuits, while observing the poet, how the power of love can be diminished by our obsessions with intellectual or activist endeavors. One

of Sanchez' most dramatic, forcefully effective prose-
poems, "Just Don't Never Give Up on Love" relates the
story of the poet busily trying to write an overdue book
review on a park bench one summer day when an old
Black woman engages her, reluctantly at first, in conversation. Full of the knowledge of life that comes from experience, the old woman becomes the essence of Black womanhood seasoned and undaunted by the failure of one marriage and by the sudden death of another husband with
whom she had a blissful marriage. The strength and power
of the old woman's love penetrates the poet's alienation
and arrogance and causes her to drop her obsession with
the book review and bask in the warmth and wisdom of an
old Black woman. When the poet says to the old woman
that she has given her courage to keep looking for love, the
old woman advises that the poet does not have to look for
love, that she must only be receptive when love finds her.
In other words, the poet must not give up on love. The old
woman's rejuvenation of the poet's communal spirit and
her alleviation of the poet's anxiety over the book review
attest to the healing power of love and the role it should
play in our lives.

"Just Don't Never Give Up on Love" introduces
Sanchez' prose-poems, a genre that captures the most
dynamic and dramatic dimension of her craft. When we
read this piece, we are consciously aware of its prose form,
but when it is read aloud, especially when it is read by
Sanchez, the differences between poetry and prose collapse
or coalesce. Clearly, Sanchez challenges the distinction
between free verse and prose. In *Free Verse: An Essay on
Prosody*, Charles O. Hartman explains that the common
charge against free verse, despite its popularity, was that it
was prose by default (13). He contends, however, that
rather than representing constituents along a spectrum, a
dichotomy exists between prose and poetry because lineation distinguishes them. Lineation causes the reader to

pause at the end of a line, and this pause forces the reader (and auditor as well) to slow down and pay closer attention to what has just been said. Lineation, then, according to Hartman, is a prosodic device that prose lacks (52). He writes: "What rhyme and meter can do [in verse], lineation alone can do" (60). While Hartman's use of lineation as the basic distinction between prose and poetry appears quite sound, his argument loses validity when applied to Sanchez' prose-poems.

In his discussion of oral narratives, Okpewho straight-forwardly asserts that "the distinction traditionally observed between prose and verse does not make much sense" (163-64). He cites a passage from G. P. Lestrade that clarifies how the distinction between prose and poetry breaks down in Bantu oral literature:

> The distinction between prose and verse is a small one....the border-line between them is extremely difficult to ascertain and define, while the verse—technique, in so far as verse can be separated from prose, is extremely free and unmechanical. Broadly speaking, it may be said that the difference between prose and verse in Bantu literature is one of spirit rather than of form, and that such formal distinction as there is is one of degree of use rather than of quality of formal elements. Prose tends to be less emotion-ally charged, less moving in content and full-throated in expression than verse; and also—but only in the second place—less formal in struc-ture, less rhythmical in movement, less metrical-ly balanced (164).

Although the African oral tradition minimizes the sig-nificant role Hartman assigns to lineation, both traditions emphasize rhythm and meter as key elements that distin-guish prose from verse. In discussing rhythm as a component of free verse, Hartman writes, "Free verse, whatever other resources it may have, is verse; and verse demands that we listen to rhythm if we want to hear what the poem has to say" (60). While Sanchez' prose-poems look like prose, the rhythmic quality of these pieces totally challenges the core of Hartman's separation of prose from poetry. Short staccato lines, polyrhythmic Black speech, and a host of metaphors and similes function together as a linguistic network with marked flexibility in cadence, stress, and inflection. Thus it is easy to imagine the first paragraph of the poem "Just Don't Never Give Up on Love" performed in a variety of ways:

> Feeling tired that day, I came to the park
> with the children. I saw her as I rounded the
> corner, sitting old as stale beer on the bench,
> ruminating on some uneventful past. And I
> thought, "Hell. No rap from the roots today.
> I need the present. On this day. This Mon-
> day. This July day buckling me under her
> summer wings, I need more than old words
> for my body to squeeze into." (10)

By collapsing the superficial dichotomies that differentiate prose from poetry, Sanchez' poetry is in the African oral tradition. Her poetry preserves the tilting vernacular rhythms and continues the technical innovation African-American poets have brought to Euro-American poetry.

Sanchez' technical skill balances the emotional content of her poetry. Three prose-poems in *homegirls* treat the pernicious effects of drugs on the development of healthy African-American minds, and show how drugs prevent wholesome relationships between African-American lovers. The pieces "Norma" and "Bubba" depict highly intelligent Black youths who live in impoverished Harlem neighborhoods that fail to provide them with the self-confidence and economic means to transcend the stifling limi-

tations of those environments. Both prose-poems illustrate
the failure of the American educational system to notice the
presence of poor Black youths and to challenge them.
While Norma is a genius in language and mathematics
and in intuiting people's fears, Bubba talked to trees and
used to think that the moon belonged to him. While in
North Carolina, he would run around to the backyard and
wait for the moon to appear; when it did he would dance a
wild dance. Both Bubba, with his creative imagination,
and Norma, the genius, drop out of school and fall victim
to drug addiction.

The endings of both prose-poems demonstrate how
the poet transforms the pain she feels for Bubba and
Norma into political activism. After years of separation
and various experiences, Norma and the poet meet near
the end of the poem. Norma tells the poet how good she
looks and acknowledges that she heard the poet had gone
to Hunter College. The poet says that Norma should have
gone to Hunter, too, for it was Norma who understood the
material while the poet just studied and received good
grades. Sanchez captures the pain she feels for Norma in
an image that represents what Norma could have been:

> And I started to cry. On that summer afternoon,
> I heard a voice from very far away paddling me
> home to
> a country of incense. To a country of red clay. I
> heard her laughter dancing with fireflies. (21)

After Norma introduces the poet to her girls, they agree to
meet again, and the poet says, "Then I pulled myself up
and turned away; never to agree again" (22). As demonstrated by the writing of the poem, the poet spends her life
disagreeing with a society that destroys women like
Norma.

By the time Bubba and the poet meet as adults, Bubba,
who, like Norma, once walked with drums beating inside

him, is saddled with two children screaming for food, a pregnant wife, and a drug habit in the face of his broken dreams. After graduation from Hunter College, the poet returns to the community and asks for Bubba. She finds him sitting in the park, "Nodding out the day. The years." Rather than separating herself from Bubba's pain, the poet identifies with it and uses it to strengthen her artistic vision: "As long as I have hands that write; as long as I have eyes that see; as long as I can bear your name against silence; I shall never forget our last talk Bubba. That September day when I sat next to you and told you my dreams and my prayers" (57). The last lines of the poem clearly explain what Sanchez sees as the purpose of her art. She says, "Bubba. Your footsteps sing around my waist each day. I will not let the country settle into the sleep of the innocent" (58). Embodying the collective psyche of her people, Sanchez, unlike the typical Euro-American poet, through her art, becomes the political voice of her people.

Sanchez' castigation of the evil effects of drugs, of a corrupt political system that encourages drug activity, of the lack of integrity in global political systems, of racism, of sexism, and of the problems between Black men and Black women is reinforced by the major themes of the African oral tradition, which Okpewho defines as love, praise, criticism, war, and death (138). The words of the persona, who promises Bubba that she will "not let the country settle into the sleep of the innocent," identifies Sanchez with the lampoon tradition in African oral literature. Although traditional African society cautioned its griots against the use of the lampoon for personal abuse or personal redress based on an untruth, the lampoon is used quite widely throughout Africa, according to Okpewho. He defines the lampoon as "a useful instrument for discouraging social evils such as theft, adultery, truancy, and general irresponsibility among young and old alike. This indeed is the real usefulness of these songs in the oral tradition: they encourage

the citizens of a society to observe proper conduct, cultivate a sense of purpose and responsibility, and issue a
warning whenever anyone or any group indulges in habits
that are detrimental to the moral health and general survival of the society" (138).   Thus Sanchez' final responses
to Norma and Bubba serve as paradigms for her entire
canon in which she, in the tradition of the lampoon, attacks
social evils and encourages society to be far more sensitive
than it is to the well-being of each member of the human
group.

Sanchez' ability to identify with the agony, disappointments, and despair African-Americans suffer does
not come without its price. The prose-poem "After
Saturday Night Comes Sunday," like "Norma" and
"Bubba," reflects the poet's intimate interest in the extremely deteriorating effect of drugs on the African-American
community. Whereas in "Norma" and "Bubba," Sanchez
uses the first-person narrative point of view, in "After
Saturday Night Comes Sunday," the most moving of the
prose-poems in homegirls, she uses the third-person narrative point of view to achieve a balance between subjectivity and objectivity, between spirituality and rationality.
Sandy, the protagonist in the poem, shares a number of
similarities with the poet: Sandy stutters, she is married to
a drug addict, and she has a set of twins. Sonia Sanchez
was once married to poet Etheridge Knight, who was
addicted to drugs. Through Sandy, Sanchez achieves the
distance necessary to give her story depth and power. The
fact that she consistently risks self-disclosure attests to the
degree of Sanchez' commitment to awaken the spiritual
and political consciousness of Black people. Kalamu ya
Salaam also comments on the value of Sanchez' adroit skill
at transforming the personal into art: "No other poet of the
1960's and 1970's managed so masterfully to chronicle
both their public and personal development with poetry of
such thoroughgoing honesty and relevant and revelatory

depth. The personal poetry is almost embarrassingly precise, albeit unsentimental, in rendering her emotional
development" (303).

Beautifully and optimistically titled, "After Saturday
Night Comes Sunday" presents the difficulties of a strong,
young woman, full of love and understanding for her husband, who continually fails in his attempts to kick his drug
habit. When Sandy discovers that her husband, Winston,
has written five checks resulting in a $300 overdraft at the
bank, she realizes that he is again on drugs. Although she
is upset about the money and worried about his addiction,
her heart does not harden against Winston but, because she
is emotionally stretched beyond reasonable limits, her
childhood stuttering returns. Unable to speak, she commu-
nicates with Winston by expressing her thoughts on paper
as she did as a child when she was embarrassed by her
stuttering. The extent of Winston's weakness is reflected in
his attempt to give Sandy morphine to help her sleep,
which, whether conscious or unconscious, is a pernicious
act that underlies his attempt to weaken her spirit. Yet,
despite his weaknesses, his lies and deception, as well as
his impotency, Sandy persists in her hope that her love will
be a source of strength for Winston. After she convinces
him to fight harder to defeat his addiction, he flushes his
drugs down the toilet. When sherry fails to soothe
Winston's pain, when he moans and writhes in agony,
when his body begins to suffer chills, Sandy takes off her
clothes and gets in bed with him and rubs her body against
his. She drifts off to sleep and wakes up to find that he is
gone. She goes out on the porch and "stood for a moment
looking out at the flat/Indianapolis/street and she stood
and let the late/nits air touch her body and she turned and
went inside."

The poet does not end this piece with a statement that
addresses her role as an artist as she does in "Norma" and
"Bubba." Maintaining an aesthetic distance that makes the

story powerful, Sanchez does not personalize Sandy's disappointment and pain. The depth of Sandy's love for
Winston and the magnitude of her pain suggest those life
experiences of a woman poet who reaches out to other
young Black women faced with the same dilemma: the battle between self-protection or self-love and the self-sacrifi-
cial love for a man too beaten to love himself. The poem
ends optimistically for both Sandy and the poet. The title
metaphorically makes the point that the Saturday nights of
Sandy's life—the days of bounced checks, drugs, celibacy,
stuttering—will be followed by Sunday, the day of peace
and rest presaged at the end of the poem. Beautifully crafted, the poem stands as a testimonial to the poet's ability to
take the Saturday nights of her life, channel them through
her imagination, and use them as spiritual gifts to awaken
the consciousness of African-Americans, especially, in this
case, African-American women. The highly sensitive, personal nature of this prose-poem presages the emotionally
charged last collection to date *Wounded in the House of a
Friend*. In a telephone interview, when asked why she
takes such risk in writing about deeply personal issues,
Sanchez says that her goal is to make Black people and the
larger group understand that what happens to her happens
to them. Consequently, for Sanchez the personal is both
universal and political (Telephone interview, 30 Mar. 1996).

The most effective means for the Black man and
woman to avoid the pitfalls of drug addiction and self-
annihilation is for them to be rooted in a firm knowledge of
their history. Sanchez skillfully uses African-American history as thematic focus and as a unifying stylistic principle.
All the poems in *homegirls* that focus on history from a general perspective or have a historical/literary figure as their
subject are grouped together in the last section of the collection subtitled "Grenades Are Not Free." Underneath this
subtitle is the italicized clause "a luta continua," which
means the struggle continues. These words were the revo-

lutionary slogan used by the freedom fighters in Mozambique, who struggled to win their independence from the Portuguese.   In all revolutionary battles, the grenades, those who are committed and take to the fore-front of change, often risk and lose their lives in the explo-sive confrontation with the powers that oppress them.   In this section Sanchez dedicates poems to Jesse Jackson, to poet and novelist Margaret Walker, (in the form of poetic letters) to South African writer Ezekiel Mphahlele, who returned to South Africa after years of expatriation, and to Martin Luther King Jr.

"MIA's (missing in action and other atlantas)" and "Reflections After the June 12th March for Disarmament" emerge as two of the poet's stronger representations of the role a knowledge of history plays in strengthening the African-American community's awareness of the orches-trated components of racial oppression.   By focusing on contemporary history, "MIA's" represents the need for peo-ple of color all over the world to recognize their connect-edness and to understand the historical foundations of the political forces that entrap and destroy their lives.   The poem takes the reader on a journey that begins in Atlanta, moves to Johannesburg, and ends in El Salvador, all the time making the point that the peoples of color in each of these parts of the world are oppressed by the same people, for the same reasons, and with the same outcome—the death of innocent children and of anyone else who defies the boundaries set for peoples of color.

Stylistically, "MIA's" recalls Robert Hayden's "Runagate Runagate," which is divided into two parts. The first part of Hayden's poem—a hodgepodge of the hopes of the runaway slave, the words of the slave owner looking for his slave, and the words from songs popular in the South in the mid-nineteenth century—begins with a series of unpunctuated action verbs that symbolize the move-ment of the runaway slave. The second part of the poem

focuses specifically on Harriet Tubman, the most renowned
runaway slave, who risked her life to lead many other
slaves to freedom.   This section interweaves African-
American folklore with Harriet's words to those whom she
led and the language of the wanted posters used by slave
owners. Similarly, "MIA's" is a montage divided into three
parts entitled "atlanta," "johannesburg," and "el salvador"
respectively. The poem has a prologue that sets the mood
and introduces a world in which the natural order of things
has been corrupted:

> this morning I heard the cuckoo bird calling
> and I saw children wandering like quicksand
> over the exquisite city
> scooping up summer leaves in enema bags
> self-sustaining warriors spitting
> long metal seeds on porcelain bricks. (72)

In the world Sanchez depicts in the poem, children
wander aimlessly in the mud of a lavish city in which they
smoke and sell marijuana. Their seeds will be wasted on
porcelain pavements or in public bathrooms. The harsh-
ness and hardness of the imagery connote the cruel reality
of the children's lives. The children of Atlanta symbolize
children of color all over the world who are exposed to
base realities that rob them of their childhood before they
have a chance to mature.

In the first part of the poem, Sanchez contrasts the
spiritually ritualistic ceremonies of cathedrals and colleges
in Atlanta with the activities of White supremist groups
responsible for the murder of Emmett Till. The poem then
abruptly shifts from these lyrical images to the colloquial
dialogue of an adult addressing a child:

> littleman. where you running to?
> yes. you. youngblood.
> touching and touched at random

running towards places where legions ride. (72)

The last two lines suggest that sexual seduction might have been one of the means used to lure the children to their death. The last part of this section which begins "heylady-carryyobagsfoyou?" uses the dialogue of the child to show how they try to earn money and to underscore their vulnerability.

Part II, "johannesburg," begins with the image of a South African policeman "squatting like a manicured mannequin" and pronouncing death sentences. The next two stanzas, dated August 18 and September 7, read like passages from a diary or a legal book and focus on the arrest and torture of Stephen Biko. The stanza dated September 13 sarcastically mocks the official announcement of Biko's death. This section, which begins "hear ye, hear ye. hear ye," echoes Hayden's technique of using the slave owners' wanted posters to demonstrate their perfidy. Sanchez uses Biko's death as a symbol of the hundreds of other South African warriors murdered in jail. She rhythmically and mockingly uses the line "we did all we could for him" to precede and follow the South African government's various explanations of Biko's death and of others who "hanged" themselves, "drowned" while drinking their supper, or "starved" themselves to death. She ends this section with the words "yebo madola/yebo bafazi," which mean come on men and women, a challenge to the readers of the poem to open their eyes to the ways in which politically grounded racial oppression is "multiplying multinationally over the world."

The final section, "el salvador," begins with the mourning signs of those who have died:

> country of vowelled ghosts.
> country of red bones
> a pulse beat gone mad
> with death. (74-75)

The phrase "vowelled ghosts" captures our attention immediately because of the contrast between vowels, which give richness and depth to the English language, and ghosts, which signify ambiguity and hollowness. As is the case with the children of Atlanta, the natural order of the people's lives in El Salvador has been disrupted by "redwhiteandblue guns splintering the/nits with glass." The birds that have "pedalled clockwise drowning their feet in clouds" warn the people in the village of the coming of American-supported troops that hypocritically speak of freedom, peace, and liberty as they kill the men of the village, rape the women, and destroy the land. The words "quiero ser libre/pues libre naci," which mean I want to be free, for I was born free, rhythmically appear throughout this section to underscore the perversion of racial oppression and imperialism.

The poem ends with a strong, direct challenge to its readers. The poet asks that the readers with a firm understanding of racial oppression take control of their lives and plant themselves in the middle of their blood with no transfusions for Reagan, Botha, Bush, or D'Aubuisson. In other words, she asks that we recognize that the policies of the leaders are aimed at sucking the life source from people of color. Only our "talk," "eyes," "thoughts," "love," and "actions" can bring "hope" and "victory." The very last line of the poem, "I want to be free," makes the connection with slavery again as the poet echoes the last line of Hayden's poem "Mean mean mean to be free."

"Reflections After the June 12th March for Disarmament" links slavery, racial oppression, imperialism, and nuclear proliferation. Manifesting the versatility of Sanchez' poetic skill, this poem has a strong oratorical style in which the poet places herself, the "I" in the poem, at the center of her message. Sanchez begins the first three-quarters of the poem with the clause "I have come," which signifies that she sees the situation she addresses in the poem as a mission that requires the immediacy and urgency of oration as opposed to the distance and indirection of lyricism and images.

Sanchez writes this poem using the technique of repetition, which she mastered in her poetry of the late 1960s. In his seminal anthology *Understanding the New Black Poetry*, Stephen Henderson refers to the wide use of repetition in Black poetry of the 1960s as virtuoso naming and enumerating, and speculates that this technique "might conceivably lie in the folk practice of riddling and similar kinds of wordplay. It may also be related to the kind of witty gesture involved in nicknaming. It is definitely related to the kind of product brand-name story that Roger Abrahams records in *Deep Down in the Jungle*, and which still flourishes in the Black community (Henderson 34). Henderson here generally identifies the African oral tradition as the source of the virtuosic use of repetition in Black poetry. Okpewho cites repetition as a central component of African oral literature. He writes, "Repetition is no doubt one of the most fundamental characteristic features of oral literature. It has both an aesthetic and a utilitarian value: in other words, it is a device that not only gives a touch of beauty or attractiveness to a piece of oral expression (whether song or narrative or other kind of statement) but also serves certain practical purposes in the overall organization of the oral performance" (70). The repetition of the words *I have come* and *I come to you* also place this poem in the tradition of the African praise poem, in which the poet situates herself at the center of the movement for disarmament. In cataloging African-American history, she at once celebrates, in the tradition of the praise poem, Black achievement and inspires or challenges her readers to rally round the fight for universal peace.

Utilizing the African praise-poem form, "Reflections After the June 12th March for Disarmament" begins by taking the reader on a journey through African-American his-

tory by enumerating influential African-American historical figures and political currents that have had significant
effect on the development of African-American lives:

> I have come to you tonite thru the
> delaney years, the du bois years, the
> b.t. washington years, the robeson
> years, the garvey years, the
> depression years, the you can't eat
> or sit or live just die here years,
> the civil rights years, the black power
> years, the black nationalist years, the
> affirmative action years, the liberal
> years, the neo-conservative years (65.)

In order for African-Americans to understand their
current place in the world, they must have a strong sense
of their history. Throughout the entire poem, Sanchez continues to place imperialism and the manufacturer of
nuclear arms at the core of slavery and racial oppression.
Her point is that these forces—imperialism, materialism,
inhumanitarianism, capitalism, and hypocrisy—that
threaten to destroy the world are the same evils responsible for the slave trade. Sanchez uses repetition not only to
give the poem a rhythmic beat and establish a structural
function but also to enhance the feeling of excitement and
urgency (Okpewho 70), and to emphasize the need for us
to strike out against those who would control the world
and amass excessive wealth. "Reflections After the June
12th March for Disarmament" emerges as one of Sanchez'
most impressive poems and presages the ingenious piece
entitled "Improvisation" in *Wounded in the House of a Friend*,
the beauty of which is also grounded in the repetition technique of the African oral tradition.

Published before *Wounded*, both *homegirls* and *Under a
Soprano Sky* bring to maturity the poet's skillful use of lyricism and images that first became apparent in the new

poems collected in *I've Been a Woman* (1978). Although many of the poems in *Under a Soprano Sky* demonstrate this pronounced development in Sanchez' poetry, "Kaleidoscope" in *homegirls* illustrates the bridge between the two collections most precisely. Because "Kaleidoscope" is a short series of interconnected images, it is necessary to quote it in its entirety:

> tumbling blue and brown
> tulips that leap
> into frogs
> women dancing in metal
> blue raindrops sliding
> into green diamonds
> turtles crawling outward
> into stars
> electric w's
> spreading beyond words
> papooses turning
> into hearts
> and butterflies stretching
> into court jesters
> who jump
> amid red splinters
> just like you.   (44)

This poem resembles a riddle in the African oral tradition. A "verbal puzzle in which a statement is posed in challenge and another statement is offered in response either to the hidden meaning or the form of the challenge" (Okpewho 238), a riddle, much like the proverb, often addresses conflicts or problems. Composed in a series of images, "Kaleidoscope" suggests a societal problem and indirectly challenges the reader to respond to the conflict at the end of the poem. Suggestive of 42nd Street in New York City or the old 14th Street in Washington, DC, "Kaleidoscope" emerges as a verbal streetscape in which neon signs reflect the glitter and unreality of the lives of the people who populate the street. By making the reader a part of the kaleidoscope, the poet implicitly provokes readers to avoid becoming court jesters, who accept whatever role society expects of them.

The pronounced change in style between *homegirls* and *Under a Soprano Sky* is marked by Sanchez' heavy use of private images. This change leads us to a more important difference between the two collections. The title *homegirls & handgrenades* is as forceful, realistic, and hardhitting as the poems in the collection. Although poems like "Kaleidoscope," "Masks," and "Depression" depend heavily on metaphors and images for their message, the majority of the poems in *homegirls* explosively and directly attack the various evils of Western society. Thus *homegirls* can be described as a *militant* collection in which the poet uses self-defense mechanisms as a means of protecting herself and warning those around her of the dangers they face. *Under a Soprano Sky*, on the other hand, through its dominant use of images that camouflage the poet's meaning and soften the directness of her earlier poetry, is a *revolutionary* collection in which the poems reflect the poet's inward movement and a desire on her part to strengthen and change herself in order to continue her struggle to change the world. This development, however, does not mean that *Under a Soprano Sky* does not continue Sanchez' condemnation of the political, economical, sociological, and psychological evils of Western society. Numerous poems in this collection demonstrate her interest in these issues. The poet alters the stylistic approach she uses to give shape and voice to these issues, an approach which suggests that she seeks an emotional respite from the aggressive, confrontational posture of her earlier poetry.

Structurally, *Under a Soprano Sky* is a more complex collection than any of Sanchez' previous volumes. With the title poem serving as prologue, the book is divided into six sections with individual poems connected by brief excerpts from such chronologically and culturally diverse figures as Bob Marley, Shakespeare, Nicolas Galen, Pablo Narrate, and Antar. Sanchez interweaves illustrations by Adjoa Jackson-Burrowes throughout the volume. These illustrations function as references for the poems they complement. *Under a Soprano Sky* also contains more haiku and tanka poems than any of her other collections since *Love Poems* (1973). Along with the title, all of these features endow this volume with the imaginative and visual qualities of a linguistic painting.

The first poem "Under a Soprano Sky," which also carries the title of the collection, best exemplifies the fecund images that give this volume its highly visual, yet enigmatic nature. The first stanza immediately demonstrates my point:

> once I lived on pillars in a green house
> bordered by lilacs that rocked voices into weeds.
> I bled an owl's blood
> shredding the grass until I
> rocked in a choir of worms.
> obscene with hands, I wooed the world
> with thumbs
>   while yo-yos hummed.
> was it an unborn lacquer I peeled?
> the woods, tall as waves, sang in mixed
> tongues that loosened the scalp
> and my bones wrapped in white dust
> returned to echo in my thighs. (3)

Very subtlely with the skill of Wallace Stevens' sleight-of-hand man, Sanchez writes a poem about a woman's loss of fertility and youth and thus about a woman's response to the process of growing old. In this first part, the woman used to live in abundance; she lived with flowers that made weeds sing; she lived a happy life. She was wise enough to make the lowest forms of life happy. Yet, with her per-

spective on the world's obscenities, she could not get those
in power to see their negative ways. While the youth (perhaps the woman's children) played with toys like the
Duncan yo-yos that used to hum, she tried to rid herself of
the false coating of that time (probably the early 1960s).
She yearns to feel the freedom, to think positively, and to be
fertile. In the last section of Part I of the poem, the woman
explains that although her feelings of youth are vague, she
would still like to feel young again. She has difficulty
accepting that she will not be young again, that she will not
give birth again.

Part II of the poem captures the essence of the poet's
feminine message and her feminine images:

> now as I move, mouth quivering with silks
> my skin runs soft with eyes.
> descending into my legs, I follow obscure birds
> purchasing orthopedic wings.
> the air late this summer.
>
> I peel the spine and flood
> the earth with adolescence.
> O who will pump these breasts? I cannot waltz
> my tongue.
> under a soprano sky, a woman sings,
> lovely as chandeliers. (3)

Thus as the woman goes about life's duties, she still
talks of love and sensuality, but "the air is late this summer." She knows that the peak of sensuality has passed
and that time has brought with it medical problems, yet she
peels the spine and flood(s) the earth with adolescence. In
other words, she continues to feel young despite the aging
process her body experiences: "O who will pump these
breasts; I cannot waltz my tongue."

The last two lines resolve the issues addressed
throughout the earlier parts of the poem. Under a soprano

sky the woman sings the song of femininity as beautifully
as when she was young. Even more dramatically than she
does in "After Saturday Night Comes Sunday," Sanchez
here achieves an aesthetic distance from her subject
through a skillful use of images much like those in Wallace
Stevens' "Sunday Morning." The voice in Stevens' poem is
that of a woman who questions the meaning of death and
religion. Stevens uses natural images to celebrate the principle of change, which governs the natural order of things.
The woman finally accepts that the answer to the nature of
life does not lie in religion, but in the principle of change
which produces the natural world. The poem ends with
the image of a bird flying "Downward but on extended
wings," an image that suggests the poet's willing acquies-
cence to the natural world. Like Stevens, Sanchez' execu-
tion of her message is imbedded in images of nature, which
question the natural cycle of life, and she, too, ends with a
metaphor that illustrates her acceptance of the principle of
change, but which also suggests a separation between the
physical self and the spiritual. The last two lines "under a
soprano sky, a woman sings/lovely as chandeliers" reflect
the poet's feeling that although she is growing old and is
not the young, attractive woman able to give birth, she is
still a spiritual woman who sings the beautiful songs of life.
A soprano voice is the song of femininity.

     This beautiful poem opens the collection and, both
stylistically and thematically, presages the poems to follow.
Although *Under a Soprano Sky* is clearly an even more eclec-
tic representation of the issues that capture Sanchez' attention than the previous *homegirls & handgrenades*, "A poem
for my brother (reflections on his death from AIDS: June 8,
1981)," "elegy (for MOVE and Philadelphia)," "Song No. 2,"
the prose-poem "Dear Mama," "Last recording session/ for
papa joe," "for Black history month/February 1986" as well
as haiku and tanku poems strongly reflect the stylistic sen-
sibility and the seasoned perspective apparent in the title

poem.

Divided into six parts—"death," "recovery (a)", "recovery (b)", "wake," "burial" and "(on) (the) (road). again"— "A poem for my brother" clearly substantiates Kalamu ya Salaam's idea that Sanchez' "personal poetry is almost embarrassingly precise, albeit unsentimental, in rendering her emotional development." Expressing her feelings through images in much the same way as she does in "Kaleiodscope" and "Under a Soprano Sky," Sanchez begins by explaining that she was sick the day her brother died: "The day you died/a fever starched my bones." In recovery she relates her consciousness to the morning sun as she recalls their childhood together when they were afraid of the dark and imagined that figures lurked about waiting to subdue them. Her feelings in "recovery (b)" are totally couched within the images of the phallic stems of the flower from which she seeks solace:

> There is a savior in these buds
> look how the phallic stems distend
> in welcome.
> O copper flowerheads
> confine my womb that I may dwell within.
>
> I see these gardens, whom I love
> I feel the sky's sweat on my face
> now that these robes no longer bark
> I praise abandonment. (9-10)

Because she sees the tie between human life and the natural world, now that she is older, she can surrender completely to the pain of her brother's death. The phallic imagery in this section also suggests one way AIDS is transmitted and how the disease symbolizes the disruption of natural order.

This inversion of natural order continues in both the wake and burial sections of the poem where the images imply that the poet does not need an account of the evils of the American Babylon. The images also suggest that Christ, the prince of tides, in this new world is the prince of boards; all order has been disrupted as "the earth is running palms." The poem ends with the poet on the road again (reading her poetry to audiences all over the world) and firmly aware of the corruption and hypocrisy in which religious conviction is bought and sold. The fact that the poet wrote the poem and that she reads it to her audiences illuminates the meaning of the last three lines,

> O I will gather my pulse
> muffled by sibilants
> and follow disposable dreams. (10)

Sanchez' use of the word *disposable* here is characteristic of her skill at using a word in a context that both surprises us and challenges our usual concept of the word's meaning. Rather than implying that the poet's dreams are useless, disposable here denotes availability. In a world so corrupt that even the structure of religion fails to protect the sanctity of human life, the poet must find strength in the dreams available to her.[1]

Although Sanchez describes a world that continues to devalue the sanctity of human life, the tone of "elegy (for MOVE and Philadelphia)" is not as somber and controlled as "A poem for my brother." Sanchez returns in "elegy" to a heightened use of the African lampoon tradition in which she castigates the political components of racial oppression through the hard-hitting sarcasm associated with her poetic voice. The focus of attack in the poem is Mayor Wilson Goode's giving the police the command to bomb the headquarters of MOVE, a nature group that wore dreadlocks and whose ideology and physical habits threatened those around them on Osage Street. The bombing, which occurred on May 13, 1985, killed men, women, and children and destroyed an entire city block. The poet begins by describing Philadelphia as a city of colleges, cathedrals, cowboys, auctioneers, and gladiators, "erasing the delirium of death from their shields/while houses burn out of control" (12). Using a technique similar to that of "MIA's," the voice in section two of the poem shifts to that of a young girl who cries out to her friend asking her to join her as she rushes down to Osage Street, where the bodies are roasting in the fire and the smell of deadlocked hair and black skin fill the air. In the fourth and fifth sections of the poem, identifying with those who died, the poet shifts to a somber voice which asks, "how does one scream in thunder?" With this question, she returns to the riddle, forcing the reader to think more deeply about the issues she raises in the poem. In sections six and seven, the poet adopts the language of a sermon to mock the self-righteousness of a people who destroy human beings merely because they look and act differently: "who anointeth this city with napalm?/who giveth this city in holy infanticide?" (13) Echoing Biblical language, she shows the hypocrisy and perniciousness of one man (the kingfisher) or a group of people (pinstriped generals) setting themselves up as gods over another group. Like the deceptively exquisite environment of cathedrals and colleges in Atlanta, section eight shows the contrast between the reckless, extravagant destruction of life in Philadelphia and the Philadelphia that tourists see characterized by concerts, football, and "mummers strutting their sequined processionals," a reference to the New Year's Day mummers' parade in which thousands of dollars are spent on paper and feathers. Although not as strong as the last lines of "Norma" and Bubba," the end of the poem manifests the poet's persistence in attacking the societal malaises that destroy human lives and stifle the human spirit:

there is this earth. this country. this city.

> this people.
> collecting skeletons from waiting rooms
> lying in wait. for honor and peace.
> one day. (14)

The poet identifies here with the friends and relatives of the deceased, collecting the bodies of their dead.

"Song No. 2" shifts the focus from the reckless destruction of life to the nature of the relationship between African-American men and women. Sanchez addresses the ways in which racism distorts and disrupts the harmony needed between African-American men and women. Rather than exacerbating the emotional chasm that already exists between African-American men and women, she speaks to both of them:

> I say, step back sisters, we're rising from the dead
> I say, step back johnnies. we're dancing on our heads
> I say, step back man, no mo hanging by a thread.
> I say, step back world, can't let it go unsaid. (80)

From *Home Coming* to *Under a Soprano Sky*, her consistent point has always been that women must develop their sense of self-respect and that this development will in turn give them the strength they need to reject unhealthy relationships with men who attempt to lure them with drugs, sex, and money. With a strong sense of self-worth, African-American women will attract men capable of building the trust and stability that make up a healthy love relationship.

The form of "Song No. 2," with its four-line stanzas and use of repetition to achieve a rhythmic effect, suggests a song. From the much earlier poems in *We a BaddDDD People* that weave song titles, lyrics, and rhythms into their fabric to the latest poems in *Wounded in the House of a Friend*, Sanchez' poetry reflects the historical importance of African-American music. Although much has been written on the connections between African and African-American music, I am not aware of any studies that examine the interrelationship of the African oral performance, the use of repetition, and music in the works of the Black writers of the 1960s. Sanchez masters repetition so adroitly that she emerges as a priestess of the African oral tradition.

While Euro-American aestheticians deemphasize or shun the use of repetition, it plays a crucial role in the structure of the African oral performance:

> If the oral performance (whether song or story) relies so heavily on these repeated devices not only to deliver a musical effect that appeals to the audience as well as the performer, but also to support the overall framework on which the performance is built, then repetition can justly be said to be a distinguishing feature of oral literature. This does not mean that one cannot find instances of repetition in written literature—essay, novel, poem, or play—either in the simplest or most complex forms. But whereas the writer generally makes every effort to avoid repetition (whether in phrase or in logic) and carefully eliminates any noticeable instances of repetition in fear that they might cause the composition to drag and so bore its readers, the oral performer cultivates repetition both as means of achieving auditory delight in listeners and as a convenient framework for holding the distinct elements of the composition together. (Okpewho 77-78)

Thus what might appear as careless repetition to those trained in a western aesthetic emerges as carefully-wrought artistry in the African oral tradition. Like the African griot, Sonia Sanchez in "Song No. 2" and in other poems, particularly "Improvisation," which appears in *Wounded*, weaves repetition into the fabric of her poems for emphasis and to achieve a rhythmic effect. Because poetry is song and repetition is an integral stylistic feature of music, it is natural that repetition would surface as a key feature of poems intended as poetic representations of music. What distinguishes Sanchez here is her success in mastering this technique, as well as the diverse ways in which she uses repetition.

"Blues" and "Song" in *homegirls* are poetic adaptations of blues and popular African-American songs respectively. "Last recording session/for papa joe" in *Under a Soprano Sky* best demonstrates the poet's idea that time has erased or dulled the memory of young African-Americans, who, because they are so far removed from their roots, are unable to perform their music with Papa Joe's natural precision. While the music was an integral part of Papa Joe's development, young musicians must work hard to learn his technique. The poet says:

> don't be so mean papa
> cuz the music don't come easily now
> don't stomp the young dude
> straining over his birthright.
> he don't know what he doing yet
> his mornings are still comin
> one at a time. (47)

Whether she writes about the dissolution of a musical tradition, the loss of a loved one to a deadly "social disease," the bombing of human communities, or the need for wholesome relationships between men and women, Sanchez always remains grounded in African-American history. Like *homegirls, Under a Soprano Sky* also includes poems that emerge as history lessons with the aim to educate and inspire the African-American community. "Dear Mama" and "for Black history month/February 1986" continue this tradition and share an affinity with "Reflections After the June 12th March for Disarmament."

Just as she does in "Reflections After the June 12th

March for Disarmament, Sanchez, with varying emphases, places the experiences of her life, her personal history, at the center of "Dear Mama" and "for Black history month." "Dear Mama" celebrates the poet's grandmother in particular and those older African-American church women in general who were responsible for shaping the poet's personality:

> And history began once again. I received it and
> let it circulate in my blood. I learned on those
> Saturday afternoons about women rooted in
> themselves, raising themselves in dark
> America...And I crept into my eyes. Alone with
> my daydreams of being woman. Adult.
> Powerful. Loving. Like them. Allowing nobody
> to rule me if I didn't want to be. (54-55)

The death of the grandmother left the poet unprotected at the age of six. Though she replaced her grandmother's love with writing poetry, it is the spirit of a long line of African-American women who gives the poet the strength and inspiration illuminated in her art: "My life flows from you Mama. My style comes from a long line of Louises who picked me up in the nits to keep me from wetting the bed...A long line of Black people holding each other up against silence" (55-56).

Strength and self-confidence instilled in her by a long line of African-American women give Sanchez the courage to challenge continually the destructive aspects of modern life and to speak up in situations where many would easily remain silent. One such incident she describes in "for Black history month/February 1986" and makes it the central focus of this prose piece, which reads like notes from a journal. In the spring of 1973, while she was visiting the People's Republic of China, her tour guide said, "Now, Professor Sanchez, we will sing one of the songs of your people—'Old Black Joe'"(95). Instead of dismissing the tour guide as incorrigibly racist and totally uninterested in the realities of African-American culture, Sanchez quickly realized that the Chinese woman was simply using the information that had been given to her by White cultural workers. Putting herself in the role of cultural teacher, Sanchez explained the stereotype represented in "Old Black Joe." This act of explaining authentic Black culture and life empowers the poet:

> My explanation prevailed because I explained how in unraveling the years of slavery and exploitation, I had to peel away misconceptions about Blacks, and at the same time gain strength from the life experiences and beauty within the culture. (95)

Calling up the spirits of Phillis Wheatley, Billie Holiday, Paul Robeson, W.E.B. DuBois, Nat Turner, Robert Hayden, Ida B. Wells Barnett, Sojourner Truth, Martin Delany, Malcolm X, Rosa Parks, David Walker, Dr. Martin Luther King Jr. and Margaret Walker reminds the poet of the centuries of work it has taken to challenge the myth of Black inferiority. The poem becomes a historical testimony to African-American survival.

Like "Bubba," "Norma," and "After Saturday Night Comes Sunday," "Dear Mama" and "for Black history month" make one seriously question the thin line that separates free verse from prose, though "Dear Mama" has stronger characteristics of prosody than does "for Black history month." In citing the passages from "Dear Mama" above, I discovered that separating the lines so that they would appear exactly as they do in the text proved impossible. In experimenting with this process, I also noticed that numerous points of demarcation were possible. Again, just as in "After Saturday Night Comes Sunday, the rhythmic Black speech serves as the core of its poetic quality. Although "for Black history month" has less of this rhythmic quality because the poet speaks in her formally educated voice rather than the communal voice she uses in "Dear Mama," "for Black history month" achieves its poetic quality through the poet's integration of a stanza from a poem by Phillis Wheatley, lines from Robert Hayden's "Runagate, Runagate," and lines from Margaret Walker's poem "For My People" into the fabric of her text. Typical of the African poetic heritage from which Sanchez writes, "for Black history month" and "Dear Mama" are both prose and poetry. They represent a new genre with a fluidity characteristic of African oral tradition that integrates theme, divination, and incantation. Since the success of these features depends heavily upon the performer's use of voice sounds, to be an accomplished poet, it is necessary that Sanchez master the technique of transcribing her electric, exciting oral performances to the written page. The fact that the listener is unable to distinguish a formal difference between her prose-poems and those that look like poetry testifies to the range of Sanchez' skill.

No discussion of Sanchez' artistic virtuosity would be complete without some discussion of her haiku poems, which she includes in *homegirls*, *Under a Soprano Sky*, and *Wounded in the House of a Friend*. In the Japanese tradition from which it comes, this seventeen-syllable poem (with the first, second, and third lines having 5-7-5 syllables respectively) is characterized by natural imagery, simple diction, assonance, alliteration, verbal dexterity, allusion, enjambment, rhythm, and rhyme (Garrets 118). Having written "Sonia Sanchez: A Continuing Journey" before the publication of Isidore Okpewho's *African Oral Literature*, I was not aware of the sharp similarities between the African proverb and haiku poetry. Entitling her poems haiku and often speaking of her fondness for this form, Sanchez herself does not make this connection. Okpekwo's description of the African proverb demonstrates that the proverb shares brevity and an enhanced imaginative quality with the haiku form:

> No doubt the most widely acknowledged stylis-
> tic quality of the proverb is its economy of
> expression. . . . Economy of expression simply
> indicates that in one statement or so, the proverb
> captures a large situation or an experience; in a
> brief, metaphorical way the proverb says what it
> would have taken many more words to say in
> direct language....Besides being economical and
> metaphorical, African proverbs have several
> other stylistic qualities which mark them out as
> literary statements. But perhaps they show their
> oral literary character best of all in the appeal
> which they make to our ears. Part of this appeal
> is achieved through the repetition of sounds in
> successive words or lines; we are referring here
> to devices of alliteration, assonance, and rhyme.
> (237-28)

Despite their differences in the number of lines
allowed their artists, the haiku and the proverb share brevity of expression, the figurative characteristics essential to
poetry, and, equally as important, the goals of arousing
emotions and/or providing insight. Sanchez takes this
Eastern form and shapes it to fit her African-American
artistic vision. This task is easy for her, however, because
her poetry naturally possesses the characteristics of the
African oral tradition. In Under a Soprano Sky, she writes,

haiku
(for domestic workers
in the african diaspora)

I works hard but treated
bad   man. i'se telling you de
truth   I full of it. (52)

Here the poet uses Black speech to symbolize the connection between Black people throughout the diaspora. At the same time that the three-line stanza satisfies the syllabic requirement for the haiku, the inflection on the verbs in the first and second lines, as well as the spacing between *bad* and *man* and between *truth* and *I*, forces the reader to read the poem with the polyrhythmic, colloquial Black speech.

Although *Under a Soprano Sky* contains many perfectly-crafted haiku poems, one other emerges as particularly interesting. She writes:

> man. you write me so
> much you bad as the loanhouse
> asking fo they money. (70)

Again her use of Black folk speech gives the poem a universally Black meaning: the speaker in the poem is quite familiar with the need to borrow money. She ironically and wryly inverts the normal order of things, comparing the person who writes to her for money to the loanhouse (that could be illegally Black or legally White) that is always quick to collect its money. Knowing that Sanchez at one time had two sons in college and realizing the frequency with which college students request money from home could add a humorous dimension to the poem. Of course, the requirements for the African proverb and the haiku—brevity, verbal dexterity, and allusion—make it quite easy for Sanchez to withhold the identity of the "man" in the poem.

In addition to the haiku, Sanchez also introduces tanka poems as early as 1978 in her collection *I've Been a Woman*. Slightly more sustained than the haiku, tankas require a total of thirty-one syllables, arranged in five lines with the first and third lines consisting of five syllables and the other lines consisting of seven syllables. In her 1995 collection *Wounded in the House of A Friend*, Sanchez, however, alters the tanka, creating her own form, which she refers to as *sonku*. Her one sonku has five lines with each line consisting of five syllables. While she is consciously inconsistent with the number of syllables she uses for the tanka and the haiku, this one sonku has a regular, or the same meter with all five lines having five syllables each. Like most of the tanka and haiku in *Wounded*, the following sonku addresses a particularly feminine issue, especially the pain women experience from betrayal or abuse:

> have mercy on the
> woman who can't hold
> her breath cuz the man's
> gon take her for a
> long ride to the deep.   (89)

Sanchez' consistent fondness for the haiku reflects the serious attention she gives to precision. Her haiku, tanka, and sonku in *Wounded* maintain the strict, skilled linguistic discipline found in the African proverb as demonstrated by the following image:

> the sprawling sound
> of my death sails on the wind
> a white butterfly.   (94)

Like an African proverb or riddle, the above haiku presents an image, a situation, a puzzle for the reader/listener to contemplate or solve. The reader's pronunciation of *sprawling* determines whether the first line has four or five syllables, and the second and third have seven and five syllables, respectively.

While a few of the poems in her previous collection *Under a Soprano Sky* depend upon images and illusions too obscure for the reader to comprehend, *Wounded* presents challenges, mysteries, and ambiguities. And rather than leaving the reader perplexed, these puzzling poems leave

us with the idea that some of Sanchez' lines must be reread
and contemplated over time. Perhaps, nothing illuminates
her peculiar shaping of language more than the title of this
latest collection. Most of us would expect to be wounded
in the house of an enemy, not in the house of a friend. In
a telephone interview, Sanchez explains that she woke up
one morning with the line "Wounded in the House of a
Friend" in her mind. Thinking that it was a line from the
Bible, she called a friend who identified the source for her
as the thirteenth chapter and sixth verse of the book of
Zechariah (30 Mar. 1996). Her use of this line as the title of
her book reflects the spiritual truths in the Bible as well as
in the African lampoon tradition against social evils.

Although *Wounded* attacks the evil in all forms of
abuse—drug addiction, oppression, poverty and other
isms—the collection spotlights the Black male's treatment
of women, women's vulnerability, and the need for women
to protect themselves against male exploitation and abuse.
The title poem "Wounded in the House of a Friend" introduces the tone and major issues of the entire volume.

A combination of prose, poetry, and drama, this
piece fulfills the mission set forth in the epigraph from
Frantz Fanon, which introduces the poem:

> I have only one solution: to rise
> above this absurd drama that
> others have staged around me. (xiii)

In this very painful poem about wounded love, deceit,
rejection, and betrayal, Sanchez gives voice to both the
betrayed woman and the deceitful man in language that is
raw, undecorated, and stripped to the bare bones, allowing
the female voice to rise from the drama strengthened with
"MEAT ON [HER] SOUL." The linguistices in Part II of
this poem is dramatically different from Part I. Labeled
"Set. No. 2," this section is a blues song in which the lay-

away man represents the betrayer and the singer, the betrayed lover. Traditionally, we have thought of the blues as a wailing chant of sadness that records a lover's defeat. In this poem Sanchez uses the blues to suggest the woman's coming to terms with the reality of her life. The betrayed lover's characterization of her lover as a layaway man and their love as an installment plan demonstrates her understanding of the insignificant role she has played in her lover's life.

Having put meat on her soul, the woman has now overcome/survived the duplicity and synchronism of her jazz-like life and reshaped or redefined herself through a blues solo. Characteristic of Sanchez, in this four-stanza set, she imprints her own style onto the typical blues form by using one traditional quatrain, descriptive of the blues, and adds to it three three-line stanzas. Four interrelated words *layaway man* and *installment plan*, which have multiple connotations, carry the meaning of the entire set and bring closure to set no. 1. Dividing the poem into sets used to describe a jazz composition, the poet calls attention to the manner in which the poem orchestrates its multiple voices (the betrayed lover's, the betrayer's, and the poet's). Linguistically, Sanchez represents this multiplicity by using regular and italic print, and, dramatically, by setting off a portion of the poem similar to dialogue in a play. Manipulating the outcome, the poet, of course, stands outside the drama.

The tone of the poem echoes the degree to which the singer has survived her pain. This tone of strength and survival along with Sanchez' unadulterated depiction of pain and anger, such as in the line "*you can't keep his dick in/your purse*," introduces the shocking honesty the reader can expect from the entire collection. The reader who makes the mistake of thinking that Sanchez is writing exclusively about her own experiences misses considerably the power and range of her creative abilities. When asked about what appears to be the deeply personal nature of her poetry, she explains that she has always written about sensitive issues, that her goal is to make the people of the larger group understand that what happens to her happens to them. She says that the situations in her poetry do not directly corresponds to the incidents in her life. She presents the "gist" of the thing and emphasizes the seriousness of the sense of loss that goes on in the world (Telephone interview, 30 Mar. 1996).

Even a cursory reading of her poetry from *Home Coming* to this new volume reveals that she has always written about the most personal of issues and confirms her idea that the personal is political. This interrelationship is nowhere more obvious than in the five occasional poems that appear in *Wounded*. In keeping with the African oral tradition in which the oral performer is commissioned to praise or record the accomplishments of the king or village, the occasional poems in this collection far outnumber those in any of Sanchez' previous volumes. Of course, the suggestion here is not that Sanchez was paid to write these poems, but that they have their origins in an African oral tradition that Sanchez contemporizes. "Catch the Fire," "On the Occasion of Essence's Twenty-fifth Anniversary," "A Love Song for Spelman," "Sweet Honey in the Rock," and "Introduction of Toni Morrison, and Others, on the Occasion of the Publication of Her Book *Race-ing Justice, En-gendering Power: Essays on Anita Hill, Clarence Thomas, and the Construction of Social Reality* emerge as far more than poems that feature the accomplishments of Bill Cosby, Susan Taylor, Johnnetta Cole, Bernice Reagan, and Toni Morrison respectively. At the core of these poems is Sanchez' condemnation of slavery and its many effects, of drug abuse, of the abuse of children, of Black-on-Black crime, of Black self-hatred, of the mental and physical abuse of women, as well as her celebration of Black women and Black life and history (in Africa and the diaspora).

Though it is typical of Sanchez to address the above range of issues, a number of the poems in Wounded emerge as far more disagreeably precise in their castigation of the abuse of women, especially the aforementioned "Wounded in the House of a Friend" and the sobering "Eyewitness: Case No. 3456." This very short prose-poem gives the vivid details of a rapist who enters a woman's home and threatens her with a knife as he rapes her. With the power of Sanchez' chants, her description of the rapist's hatred of his victim forbids the reader's neutrality:

> Don't you look at me he screamed as he moved
> the knife toward my vagina.
> Don't you open yo mouth or yo eyes or you
> dead. Bitch. Bitch. Bitch. Yes.
> Bitch. Bitch. Blk mothafucking bitch.   (69)

While some surely are repulsed by Sanchez' use of profanity, others of us understand that Sanchez and other Black poets, especially those who began writing in the 1960s, use profanity to depict the reality that underlie the feelings that motivate us.

From the first line of this prose piece, which begins "I was raped at 3 o'clock one morning," to the end where the raped woman runs out of her house with blood running down her legs, this prose-poem challenges both male and female readers' ability to discipline their passion to the same degree that the poet disciplines hers. Because the poet has the rapist speak in his own voice, prose provides her with the flexibility to allow the rapist to reveal his true nature through his own dialogue:

> This is. . . . This is. . . . This is the best. . . . This is
> the best
> fuckin ever man. Fuck. Cmon man do it do it do
> it yes. That's it feels good oh it feel so good.
> Fuck me. Fuck me, fuck me hard, fuck me, fuck

me.... Oh my God, Oh my God....   (70)

When asked about the deeply personal and highly sensitive nature of this poem, Sanchez responds, "No one says out loud you shouldn't mess over people. Messing over people is a nonrevolutionary act. If you fuck over women, fuck your wife, this is a political act; taking a child into a crack house is also a political act" (Telephone interview, 30 Mar. 1996).

Sanchez' reference to "taking a child into crack house" alludes to the subject of the "Poem for Some Women" in which an addicted mother, desperate for a fix, in exchange for drugs, leaves her seven-year old daughter in a crack house where she is consistently raped by several men for days before the mother returns for her. Her referring to this incident as a political act is inherent in the title of the poem. Though the title makes it clear that drug addiction accompanied by the most reprehensible acts is the problem of *some* women, the content of the poem strongly suggests that drug addiction and the woman's total disregard for her child's well being is the problem of us all.

Particularly in *Wounded*, the prose-poems confirm Sanchez' position on the communal nature of human society and the role she believes the writer can play in encouraging people to take responsibility to correct social and political ills. "A Remembrance" records the poet's reaction to James Baldwin's death, and affirms Baldwin s contribution in raising the political consciousness of readers all over the world. "Homegirls on St. Nicholas" and "Nicaraguan Journal" demonstrate that Sanchez follows the tradition of her mentor Baldwin by addressing the pain and horror people face throughout the world, particularly in New York and Nicaragua.

Anyone who has heard Sanchez read her poetry on several occasions knows that each reading presents a different performance of a poem to affect her audience's emotions so that they might move beyond pain and fear to action. These variations in Sanchez' performances verify Okpewho's assertion that "an oral poem is not composed *for* but *in* performance" (68). "Improvisation" in *Wounded* proves to be a perfect example of Sanchez' success in moving back and forth expertly from the written to the oral and thus of her ability to imprint an oral quality on the written word. When she performs or chants this piece, as she does with others of her poems such as "Letter to Dr. Martin Luther King," "MIA's," "Kwa mama zetu waliotuza," "Poem for July 4, 1994," and "elegy (for MOVE and Philadelphia)," her entire body performs in her reading.

Sanchez' spellbinding performances, in which her body and voice are equally important as her words, are reflections of her conception of jazz music, which she defines as "cultural music that comes out of our lifestyles" (Telephone interview, 30 Mar. 1996). The power of her performance has its source in the African oral tradition, in which "there is a clearly marked difference between the speech voice and the chanting voice. The latter is marked by a higher degree of stress in such a way as to achieve greater emotional intensity than in normal conversational speech...the tone of chanting is frequently quite high, the chanter's aim being to impress the audience of the open performance not only with the strength and sonority of the voice but also with the importance of the idea" (Okpewho 131).

Anyone who has heard Sanchez read/perform "a/coltrane/poem" from *We a BaddDDD People* (1970) and "Improvisation," which appears in the recent *Wounded in the House of a Friend* (1995), has experienced her ability to use her voice to incite the emotional response she needs to force the reader to feel the truth of the ideas she addresses in her poems. The differences between "a/coltrane/poem" and "Improvisation" illuminate the twenty-five years Sanchez has used to improve her skill. Stylistically, these poems are very similar in their use of typography to approximate the rhythm of the jazz musician's horn. Yet, while "a/coltrane/poem" is visibly loosely scattered all over the page, "Improvisation" is tight and elongated, and uses repetition to achieve rhythm as in the following lines:

> It was the coming
> It was the coming that was bad
> It was it was it was the coming across the ocean
>   that was bad (75)

This five-page poem contains (approximately) only sixty-two different words, quite few considering that it is quite easy to put at least one hundred different words on a single page. In these few words, the poet relives the experience of slavery and affirms Black survival in the past, present, and future as exemplified in the line "I was I shall be I was I am." Just as the Black experience is diachronic and synchronic, the style of the poem connects "Improvisation" to the virtuosic use of repetition and enumeration that characterize the African oral tradition and the Black poetry of the 1960s. The fluidity and innovative quality of "Improvisation" illustrate Sanchez' use of jazz music and technique for achieving rhythm in her poetry. She says that she "wanted to bring people into a jazz situation, using language to replace music," to achieve the rhythm of pain and humor. In reference to the title of her poem, she says, "Life is improvisation" (Telephone interview, 30 Mar. 1996).

Underneath the title of the poem, she writes, "*At the Painted Bride with Khan Jamal.*" She explains that Lamont Steptoe, director of one of Philadelphia's well-known art centers, asked her and percussionist Jamal to perform a mixed media piece together. Jamal suggested that they try an improvisational piece. The poem, which she titles "Improvisation," is the result of Sanchez' transcription of a tape of that performance. Sanchez' performance of the poem and the words to the poem emphasize how Black people have made themselves. Following the tradition of the chanting African oral performer, she relives the experiences of Black people taken from Africa through the Middle Passage to a land full of oppression. Calling on Olokun, the Yoruba goddess of the sea, the poet defines who she is and who her people are: "Can't you see who I am huh/Don't you know who I am" (78). In the line "Every nine months, every nine months," which she repeats twice, Sanchez particularizes the female situation, emphasizing the fact that it is the women who are the progenitors who give birth to a strong line of African people, represented linguistically in the poem by the repeated use of various forms of the verb *to be* and by the present participial forms of various verbs.

While it is interesting that Sanchez' poems do not overtly or explicitly use the word Black to describe the women or feminine issues she addresses in *Wounded*, the voice throughout this collection is Black, identifiable through Sanchez' use of Black speech, which dominates her entire canon. However, by not directly using the descriptive word *Black*, Sanchez signals, perhaps, her awareness that all women can identify with the feelings and situations she describes. From *Home Coming* published in 1969, to *Wounded* twenty-six years later, Sanchez has been most consistent, like the African griot, in charting the history of Black people's lives and using her art to awaken our political consciousness and help us find ways to acknowledge our pain and heal it. The fact that her poetry appeals to women and male readers of all colors or nationalities testifies to her success in helping us understand that racism and other isms, such as sexism, impact on all our lives. Yet, she never compromises her Blackness nor yields to Euro-American definitions of the aesthetics of poetry. Whether one reads her dramas, such as *The Bronx is Next* or *Sister Son/ji* or her poems for children, a deeply rooted African spirituality pervades her canon from the late 1960s

to the late 1990s. In addition to its spirituality, the aesthetics of her poetry include a virtuosic manipulation of Black
speech and Black music, and a commitment to condemn-
ing political corruption. Any reading of her poetry or
attendance at her performance takes us on a spiritual and
aesthetic journey back to Africa and provides us with the
power to transform our lives.

In her thirty years of publishing poetry, Sanchez has
never sacrificed her skill for political commitment. The
range of her artistic diversity demonstrates the time she
has spent perfecting her poetic technique. Her
haiku/proverbs, her interweaving epigraphs throughout
the fabric of her book, her use of Spanish and African languages that give her work multicultural grounding, her
alternating use of italic and regular print to highlight her
poignant messages, her strongly evocative images, and the
skillful, virtuosic use of repetition coalesce to make
Wounded Sanchez' most artistic creation to date. Her eight
collections of poetry demonstrate a characteristic balance
between the personal and private, simplicity and depth,
ethics and aesthetics, spirituality and rationality. In the tradition of the well-trained African oral performer, she
merges perfectly the career of literary artist and political
activist. Although her poetry has already found a secure
place in the annals of African-American literature, no
knowledge of the depth, power, and range of Sanchez'
artistic vision would be complete without the
listener/reader hearing her sing, chant, moan, or cry, while
calling on the spirits of the ancestors to retrieve a connection to an African oral tradition.

NOTES

1. Sanchez has recently submitted her latest book manuscript to her editor at Beacon Press. Entitled "Does Your House Have Lions?," it is an epic poem in rhyme royal that explores her brother's birth, life, and death. With Wolof words dispersed throughout the book, "Does Your House Have Lions?" is a praise-poem of a Black family in which the members reconcile with each other. In the poem, the voices of the brother, sister, mother, father, male and female ancestors are heard (Telephone interview, 24 Aug. 1996).

WORKS CITED

Garrets, Joan. *The Haiku Form*. Rutland, Vermont: Charles E. Tuttle Company, 1974.

Hartman, Charles O. *Free Verse: An Essay on Prosody*. Princeton: Princeton U P, 1980.

Okpewho, Isidore. *African Oral Literature: Backgrounds, Character, and Continuity*. Bloomington: Indiana U P, 1992.

Salaam, Kalamu ya. "Sonia Sanchez.". In *Dictionary of Literary Biography*, Volume 41: Afro-American Poets Since 1955. Ed. Trudier Harris and Thadious Davis. Detroit: Gale Research Company, 1985.

Sanchez, Sonia. *homegirls & handgrenades*. New York: Thunder's Mouth Press, 1984.

_____. *Under A Soprano Sky*. Trenton, New Jersey: Africa World Press, 1987.

_____. *Wounded in the House of a Friend*. Boston: Beacon, 1995.

EPILOGUE

This book is dedicated to Dudley Randall, Gwendolyn Brooks, and Margaret Walker. Thus in now addressing their influence on Sanchez in this final chapter, *Ijala: Sonia Sanchez and the African Poetic Tradition* comes full circle. The elders in the African-American poetic tradition, Randall, Brooks, and Walker represent the strongest connection between the African griot and contemporary African-American poetry. In his seminal outline of the elements that make up a Black Aesthetic, Larry Neal places the folk poet, philosopher, priest, priestess, conjurer, preacher, teacher, hustler, seer, and soothsayer in the neo-mythology category with its roots in spirit worship and the orishas [sic] (12). "Energy that...represent [s] aspects of nature "(Neimark 14), the orisa are also referred to as Yoruba gods. Consequently, Neal, one of the most important theoreticians of the Black Arts Movement, suggests that the poet's role in the African-American community is reflective of the role the priest or medicine man plays for his/her people.

While Randall, Brooks, and Walker would certainly shun any suggestion that they be viewed as literary gods, they are indeed the elders in the African-American literary community, and their contributions have influenced generations of writers both inside and outside of the African-American community. And in keeping with the African tradition to which Larry Neal refers, these writers hold an exalted position at the head of the African-American literary family. In describing the role of elders in the African community, John S. Mbiti's *African Religions and Philosophy* makes it clear that elders frequently played the same role as priests in the traditional African community:

> We must take note of ritual leaders of different
> kinds in every African community. Households
> are generally led and represented by the head of
> the family, whether male or female, in making
> family offerings, libation and prayers. Each com-
> munity has elders or other recognized leaders
> who take charge of communal rites, ceremonies,
> weddings, settlement of disputes, initiations,
> festivals, rites of passage, rainmaking cere-
> monies, cleansing ceremonies, upkeep of shrines
> and sacred objects and places, and appoint-
> ments, or various other functions of the commu-
> nity. These are "priestly" duties, even if the offi-
> ciating persons may not be called "priests" in the
> narrow sense of the word. . . . (184)

In their role as historians, teachers, and guides, Randall, Brooks, and Walker have all, like African griots and priests, for at least four decades, produced poetry that reflects the continuity of African-American thought and history. Serving as spiritual guides for Sanchez, Randall, Brooks, and Walker function as intermediaries between Sanchez and her African ancestors.

Because Black writers in the late 1960s and 1970s struggled consciously to establish a connection between their works and an African ancestry and because they thus challenged all the aesthetic rules of the Eurocentric estab-lishment, Black poets who identified with the Black Arts Movement could not easily expect the mainstream press to publish their books. The founder of Broadside Press in 1965, Dudley Randall emerges as the elder or priest, who created a depository for African-American letters at a crit-ical time in African-American literary history. In his Broadside Series he published either the books or single poems of such writers as Etheridge Knight, Haki Madhubuti (then Don L. Lee), Sarah Webster Fabio, Askia

Toure, Carolyn Rodgers, Nikki Giovanni, Sterling Plumpp, Sonia Sanchez, and many others.

Dudley Randall published Sanchez' first two collections of poetry, *Home Coming* (1969) and *We a BaddDDD People* (1970). While Haki Madhubuti writes the introduction to *Home Coming*, Randall himself writes the introduction to the longer collection *We a BaddDDD People*. Far more of a stylistically traditional poet than Sanchez, Randall refers to some aspects of Sanchez' performance as "inarticulate screams." He appreciates the fact that Sanchez' Blackness, as he describes it, cannot be bought. He explains, "A nationally known critic advised her to let a 'professional' publisher do her next collection of poetry. Sonia commented, 'The critic don't know that Broadside Press is the ba-a-dest motherfucken press today'" (10). Sanchez' exclamatory response underscores her recognition of the fact that most White publishers would not publish works that illuminate the evils of imperialism and racism with the fervor and clarity of those of the writers of the Black Arts Movement. By publishing these works that awaken Black- political consciousness, Randall serves the same function as the formally, trained priest, who is the intermediary between Sanchez and her audience and who aids Sanchez in establishing a link with her African ancestry.

A historical link, of course, connects Dudley Randall, Gwendolyn Brooks, and Sonia Sanchez. Randall's Broadside Press also published at least two books that are now collector's items associated with Gwendolyn Brooks: *Jump Bad: A New Chicago Anthology* (1971) and *a capsule course in Black Poetry Writing* (1975), by Gwendolyn Brooks, Keorapetse Kgositsile, Haki Madhubuti, and Dudley Randall. Gwendolyn Brooks also influenced poet Etheridge Knight, whom she discovered writing poetry in prison. Knight was Sanchez' husband for a short number of years. Sanchez captures in the poem "sunday/evening

at gwen's," which appears in *We a BaddDDD People*, the
effect Brooks had on her and Etheridge Knight in the late
1960s.

Explaining that she and Knight went to Gwendolyn
Brooks' home to read their poetry, Sanchez ends the poem,

> & we came that day
>   to read our work
>   but left
>   knooowing
>   hers.   (58)

These last lines reflect Sanchez' talent for understatement.
Of course, the implications here are not only that Sanchez
and Knight have been exposed to Brooks' poetry, but also
that they have grown or been changed by their exposure to
the poet and her works.

Sanchez' connection with poet and novelist Margaret
Walker emerges as more contemporary and more sustained
than her relationship with Randall and Brooks. Walker is
the subject of "Poem for Margaret Walker," which appears
in *homegirls & handgrenades* and which beautifully demonstrates how Sanchez pays tribute to her elders and her
African ancestors. The poem sets the time period and
describes Walker's appearance at a Chicago hotel as a
speaker for a Black feminist conference. Emphasizing
Walker's strength and her Black femininity, Sanchez puts
Walker in the tradition of a long line of African women: "i
fold myself/into her and hear a primordial black song sail-
ing down the guinea coast" (60). Following these lines, the
poem becomes a descriptive tribute to Walker's poetic contributions and includes the final stanza from Walker's signature poem "For my people." Walker's poem not only
challenges Black people to follow the generation before
them and take control of their own lives, but it also celebrates the endurance and strength of a history of Blacks

who have sacrificed their lives. The last lines of Sanchez'
poem to Walker solidifies the connection between Sanchez,
the poet, and their African women ancestors:

> walking back to my room, i listen to the after-
> noon. play it again and again. scatter myself
> over evening walls and passageways wet with
> her footprints. in my room i collect papers.
> breasts, and listen to our mothers hummmm-
> ming   (60)

Given the spiritual and political nature of Sanchez' poetry,
her appreciation of Walker and her poem that challenges a
"race of men [to] rise and take control" of their lives is quite
appropriate.

Sanchez identifies Walker as an elder in the tradition
of griots, priests, priestesses, teachers, and guides, who are
the spiritual healers as well as the historians in their community. Among numerous other poets, Sanchez emerges
as a contemporary griot who, particularly like Gwendolyn
Brooks, is extremely mindful of and skilled at the oral presentation of her poetry. Because Sanchez consciously
weaves African languages, allusions to Africa, and African
stylistic features into the fabric of her poetry and because
her poetry is overtly political, her connection to the African
poetic tradition is stronger than Randall's, Brooks', or
Walker's. The differences between the works of these writers who began to publish before the 1960s and Sanchez'
poetry parallel John Mbiti's explanation of the differences
in African religions. He says, "A great number of beliefs
and practices are to be found in any African society. These
are not, however, formulated into a systematic set of dog-
mas which a person is expected to accept. People simply
assimilate whatever religious ideas and practices are held
or observed by their families and communities. These traditions have been handed down from forebearers, and each
generation takes them up with modification suitable to its

own historical situation and needs" (3).

Because art, religion, and politics were so integrally connected in traditional African society, the *ijala* poet embodies the cultural memory of his/her people. Rather than totally ignoring the contributions of their African-American elders, Sanchez and her peers in the Black Arts Movement transformed or modified what they learned from Langston Hughes, Dudley Randall, Gwendolyn Brooks, Margaret Walker, Robert Hayden, and others. While dialect, urban Black speech (*bantu*), politics (*nkodi*), music (*ndungu*), and religion (*nganga*) describe the history of African-American poetry, the degree to which these characteristics manifest in Sanchez' work distinguishes her in the African-American poetic tradition. And the most prominent example of Sanchez' modification of traditional African-American poetry appears in her oral performances. The confessional, incantatory nature of her performance/chant is difficult to match. Yet, her reputation as a writer will not rest on her performance of her poetry. Her well-established, secure place in the history of African-American letters has its roots in her adroit ability to move back and forth (interchangeably) from the oral to the written with virtuosic skill.

WORKS CITED

Mbiti, John S. *African Religions and Philosophy.* London: Heinemann, 1969. Rpt. 1990.

Neal, Larry. "Some Reflections on the Black Aesthetic." *In The Black Aesthetic.* Ed. Addison Gayle. 1971. NY: Doubleday, 1972.

Neimark, Philip John. *The Way of the Orisa: Empowering Your Life Through the Ancient African Religion of Ifa.* NY: HarperCollins, 1993.

Sanchez, Sonia. *Home Coming.* Detroit: Broadside Press, 1969.

_____. *We a BaddDDD People.* Detroit: Broadside Press, 1970.

_____. *homegirls & handgrenades.* NY: Thunder's Mouth Press, 1984.